MARINE PAINTING IN HULL THROUGH THREE CENTURIES

by Arthur G. Credland

Hull City Museums and Art Galleries
and Hutton Press
1993

Published by Hull City Museums and Art Galleries
and the Hutton Press Ltd.
130 Canada Drive, Cherry Burton, Beverley
East Yorkshire HU17 7SB

Typeset and printed by
Image Colourprint Ltd.,
Anlaby, Hull.

ISBN 1 872167 45 4

Frontispiece:
HMS Britannia, *a first rate of 120 guns, bow port side view (13 x 9 in.),*
lithographic print by John Ward, c.1842.

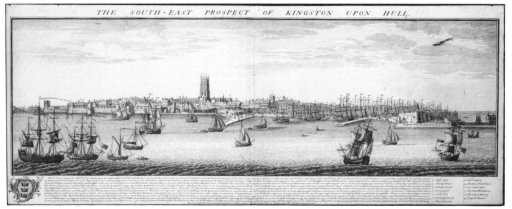

THE SOUTH-EAST PROSPECT OF KINGSTON UPON HULL.

The South-East prospect of Kingston upon Hull; Samuel and Nathaniel Buck, 1745. It shows the 'Old Harbour', the entrance to the River Hull, crowded with shipping and a large variety of craft in the Humber Roads.

A plan of the town of Kingston upon Hull, from an actual survey, 1784; drawn by J. Bryant, engraved by R. Thew. It shows the new dock and the new streets developed to the north and west. The rest of the town wall was swept away by the construction of the Humber and Princes Docks.

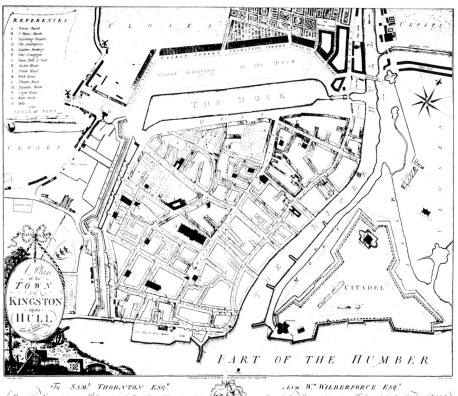

CONTENTS

PREFACE 4

FOREWORD 5

ACKNOWLEDGEMENTS 6

INTRODUCTION 7

ORIGINS AND PROGRESS OF MARINE PAINTING IN HULL 12

Thomas FLETCHER and his Kinsmen 29

Robert WILLOUGHBY and his Kinsmen 33

William BARTON 39

The MEGGITT Workshop; Thomas BINKS 42

William GRIFFIN and Reuben GRIFFIN 50

John WARD 56

William Frederick SETTLE 78

Henry REDMORE 88

Edward King REDMORE 103

James WHELDON 107

William Daniel PENNY 113

James and George WHELDALE 116

Richard Dodd WIDDAS 117

Samuel Henry WILSON 120

Thomas LUCOP and Charles LUCOP 124

Benjamin TINDALL 126

William Robert NIXON 128

Thomas Jacques SOMERSCALES 131

Harry Hudson RODMELL 134

Allanson HICK 144

Colin VERITY 149

J. Steven DEWS 153

David BELL 156

Colour Plates 159

A DIRECTORY OF MARINE ARTISTS 199

ART EXHIBITIONS in HULL 1827 - 1900 216

IMPORTANT SALES OF WORKS OF ART IN HULL 1843 - 87 217

SOURCES 218

PREFACE

It is with great pleasure that I accepted the invitation to contribute a preface to this book.

My family has long been associated with Hull and it is exactly 100 years ago that my Grandfather first opened his business here. Subsequent generations of the family including myself have an abiding affection for the City. My childhood was spent almost within sight of the then busy Humberside waterfront and our business has for so long been part of the industrial and maritime scene.

My contribution to this magnificent publication by Arthur Credland of the Hull Marine Artists provided me with a wonderful opportunity to help celebrate our centenary year.

I am sure that the volume will provide the reader with many insights into the richness and variety of artistic life which has always flourished in our great city.

Malcolm Shields

4

FOREWORD

Hull is proud of the marine artists who lovingly depicted its river-front, docks and shipping, artists who, after some neglect, are now valued and held in esteem not only for their record of technical detail but also for their craftsmanship, skills and sensitivity to the changing maritime scene.

The first attempt to produce a catalogue of these artists was made by Vincent Galloway, Curator of the Ferens from 1928-1960, in connection with the exhibition organised as part of the celebration for the Festival of Britain, 1951. Since then, some paintings have been lost from sight, but the collections at both the Ferens Art Gallery and the Town Docks Museum have grown, and Arthur G. Credland, Keeper of Maritime History for Hull City Museums and Art Galleries, has been indefatigable in searching out biographical and technical details about the artists and their product.

He produced separate catalogues for a number of the major Hull artists, John Ward in 1981, Henry Redmore in 1987, and recently for the architect artist, Allanson Hick. It is intended that further exhibitions will be devoted to specific artists and specific themes.

The re-opening of the Ferens and its new extension has allowed us to refurbish the upper floor to show the history of Hull in its marine paintings in one gallery and the Diploma Collection of the Royal Society of Marine Artists, including works by a number of local members, in the other.

It seemed therefore an appropriate occasion to launch Mr Credland's latest venture. Fortunately this occurred at the time Mr Malcolm Shields was looking for a means of commemorating the anniversary of the foundation of his firm in keeping with his own interest in collecting the works of the Hull marine painters. We are therefore indebted to him for a large investment in the present volume and to Hutton Press for undertaking the publication.

Hull City Council is well aware of the importance of its Museums and Art Galleries, in preserving the past and promoting an awareness of its maritime heritage. Mr Credland has devoted much service to the theme and added considerably to the stock of our knowledge. We hope that this systematic publication of the information he has assembled will draw attention to other works as yet unrecorded and also lead to further interest in our city, its colourful past and optimistic present.

Trevor P. Larsen
Chairman
Hull City Cultural Services Committee

John Bradshaw
Curator of Museums & Art Galleries

ACKNOWLEDGEMENTS

First and foremost the author acknowledges the generosity of Malcolm Shields whose appreciation of the local tradition of marine painting is of long standing. It is hoped that the present publication will do justice to the many fine painters active in and around the city over the last three centuries and make their work known to a wider public.

In addition, the Hull Maritime Society have enabled new photographs to be made, expertly prepared by Richmond and Rigg, of many of the pictures reproduced in this volume, a considerable proportion of which are published for the first time.

Mr. John Bradshaw, Curator of Hull Museums and Art Gallery, has given his full support and help has been forthcoming from my colleagues, Ann Bukantas, Sarah MacDonald and Tom Bucknall. Charles Brook of the Hutton Press has smoothed the path of publication and ensured the highest standards of production.

Research on the Hull marine artists has been undertaken over the past fifteen years whenever time has been available. Jill Crowther and the staff of the Local Studies Library have provided constant support in an efficient, friendly fashion and many individuals too numerous to mention have made a contribution to my investigations. Sincere thanks, however, must be offered to the following: the Wardens and Brethren of the Hull Trinity House, James Starkey, John Simpson, Ray and John Hawley, Janet Tierney, Sam Davidson, Alex Hurst, Ralph Hyde, N.R. Omell, Oscar and Peter Johnson, G.S. Yates and the staff of Messrs. Christies and Sothebys.

It is a pleasure to record a continuing and very active tradition of marine painting and thanks are also due to the present day artists who answered my numerous enquiries, in particular David C. Bell, Steven Dews and Colin Verity.

The brunt of the typing was ably tackled by Mrs. Anne Lamb of the museum staff, and my wife Mary showed immense forebearance in the weeks of preparation.

Town Docks Museum, Autumn 1992. A.G.Credland.

INTRODUCTION

The marine painters of the late eighteenth and early nineteenth century, certainly outside of London, in common with their contemporaries in other fields of artistic endeavour had no means of learning the rudiments of their profession by instruction in any formal school or institution. In all major towns there were of course a variety of resident drawing masters but they earned their living largely by teaching the wives and daughters of the rich merchants, landed gentry and professional men. On occasion an aspiring artist might have taken a lesson or two from one of these individuals but a young man without means would not be able to afford the necessary fees. The skills of all the native marine painters of this period were generally based on apprenticeship with a house or ship painter, the two trades often being combined. Occasionally a period of sea service or a stint in one of the maritime trades such as shipbuilding may have preceded such an apprenticeship.

The work undertaken by these artisan painters involved the interior and exterior painting of shops and houses both humble and grand. Their training would start with learning how to grind and mix pigments and proceed to painting, including sign-painting and sign-writing, varnishing and maybe gilding. Ship-painters applied their mops to the timbers of the fleets of merchant traders and whaling vessels, the decoration of the cabins as well as colouring and gilding figureheads and ships fancywork.

Julius Caesar Ibbetson who eventually was to establish himself as a landscape artist was bound to John Fletcher a Hull ship painter and the frustrations of the young mans ambitions are recorded by Joseph Farington the diarist 'his occupation was only . . . painting

Detail of the Birds-Eye View of Hull, a lithographic print published by F. N. Pettingell in 1881. The Town Docks system links the Humber with the Hull and timber yards and shipbuilding have taken the place of the citadel.

from daylight to night the inside and outside of ships in the port of that town. His remonstrances against this were ridiculed by his master and he could only practise drawing and other painting at stolen hours. He did, notwithstanding, so far advance in the art to paint several signs which were much admired'. [1]

He may have found his daily tasks a drudge but he would at least have gained a practical knowledge of the preparation and handling of oils and colours. Ibbetson also undertook scene-painting for Tate Wilkinson, a Yorkshire theatrical impresario, which would have given him some chance of free artistic expression.[2] A number of painters including outstanding marine artists like Clarkson Stanfield benefited from such an opportunity. [3]

Thomas Fletcher the son (or grandson) of John Fletcher is Hull's first identifiable marine painter and although only a single canvas has been discovered it is clear that he was a very able painter of ship-portraits. Robert Willoughby, the son of John Willoughby, a jobbing painter who seems to have painted landscapes, portraits and genre pieces, was particularly prolific. Predominant among his output are pictures of vessels of the Hull whaling fleet and he was particularly fortunate that his active years coincided with the great boom in the Arctic fishery. An accumulation of the particular skills and knowhow required for this particular branch of painting passed to John Ward one of the outstanding marine painters of the century who was certainly influenced by Willoughby but was apparently apprenticed to Meggitt, a house and ship painter. Thomas Binks and William Griffin, two able ship-portrait painters also served their time in the workshop of Thomas Meggitt who seems to have retained Griffin for a number of years to produce ship pictures for sale on commission. A variety of lesser lights active in the middle and latter half of the century seems to have been largely self-taught and developed only a rudimentary technique enabling them to produce works of sufficient merit only for clients lower down the social scale. [4]

The patrons of the eighteenth and early nineteenth century probably regarded most artists as little more than artisans. Portrait painters however tended to be in higher esteem than landscape artists and genre painters probably because of necessity their relationship with their clients was more intimate than was generally the case. Even so, it was really only the likes of Joshua Reynolds and Thomas Gainsborough, artists who had access to the great magnates and members of the royal family, who really achieved a sound professional and social status. [5]

John Ward established himself among the Hull Freemasons and was a member of a lodge which included many master mariners and shipowners among its number. This was an ideal way of meeting potential patrons and as a brother, then master, of the Humber Lodge his social standing was confirmed, at least within the city of Hull. Of the earlier generation Thomas Fletcher was also active as a mason, the first Junior Warden of the Rodney Lodge and a founder member of the Minerva Lodge in 1782.

The founder members of the Royal Academy included Dominic Serres as one of their number, a Gascon by birth he settled in England after being captured by a Royal Navy Frigate while in command of a trading vessel. He gained increasing Royal Patronage and a few weeks before his death was appointed marine painter to his majesty King George 3. Another founder member was Charles Catton the royal coach painter indicating that patronage could elevate the practitioners of even the more humble aspects of painting. [6]

Reynolds was the first president of the Royal Academy the first society of artists which provided tuition in the art of drawing, painting and sculpture and a means of regularly exhibiting their work to the public. Founded in 1768 its aims and objectives were not to be pursued in the provinces for many years to come. This is not surprising since it was not until the turn of the century that most provincial towns had sufficiently developed economically and with enough potential patrons to support a body of local artists who might then be able to organise and promote themselves. The Norwich Society was formed in 1804 when it was realised that the Royal Academy was essentially confined to artists working in London. Edinburgh and Bath followed in 1808, the former of course Scotland's capital city and the latter a spa town and centre of fashion. The Northern Society was formed at Leeds in 1809, Liverpool followed suit in 1810 and within the next twenty years there was a flood of provincial societies including Hull, Manchester, Birmingham, Bradford and Newcastle. [7]

The artists themselves were mainly looking for regular exhibitions which would be a showcase for their work and enable them to improve their chances of sales. Often however the prime movers of these societies were gentlemen who encouraged fine art but who chiefly saw it as a means of supporting commerce and industry. There aims were to improve arts and manufactures, to harness the arts to develop better quality products, an approach which reached its apotheosis in the Great Exhibition held at the Crystal Palace in 1851.

A school of art, direct ancestor of the present Hull College of Art was eventually opened in 1861 to teach applied art and industrial design. It started life in the Public Rooms before transfer near to the Royal Institution which had become a major contributor to adult education. The RI in Albion Street housed the rooms of the Literary and Philosophical Society and their museum as well as the Hull Subscription Library.[8]

The Hull and East Riding Institution for the Promotion of the Fine Arts established in 1827 was led by Dr. John Alderson, John Broadley, FSA, and W. H. Dikes. Alderson born in Lowestoft had originally come to Hull as surgeon with the Norfolk Militia but stayed to make outstanding contributions both in the field of medicine, especially as a founding father of the Hull Infirmary, and in the arts. He was active on the committee of the Hull Subscription Library, 1788-1807 (president 1795-1800), and the main stimulus behind the formation of the Hull Literary and Philosophical Society in 1822 and the Mechanics Institute in 1825. Broadley was president of the committee of management and the Rev. George Lee, editor of the *Hull Rockingham* newspaper was his vice-president. Samuel Talbot Hassel, merchant, was treasurer and William Hey Dikes, shipbuilder, was secretary. In addition to Dr. Alderson the committee

was made up of J. C. Cankrien, merchant and Netherlands consul, Charles Frost, FSA, solicitor and notable local historian, Thomas Ward Gleadow, brewer and maltster, John Cowham Parker, wine and spirit merchant, John Crosse, FSA, a Russia merchant, George Fielding, surgeon and Daniel Sykes MP, barrister and Recorder of Hull. The judges were Dr. C. R. Alderson (son of John Alderson); Edward Gibson, shipbuilder, Richard Tottie, merchant and American consul and H. C. Sherrin, surgeon. [9]

The first exhibition was shown at the Assembly Rooms (Public Rooms) North Street and included a variety of works by both local artists and those from out of town, as well as pieces lent by local patrons and collectors. A shilling a head was charged which with 1327 admissions left a favourable balance after the payment of expenses. There was no exhibition the following year but a second presentation took place in 1829 when the principals remained substantially the same except that W. Richardson, wine merchant and H. C. Sherrin replaced Tottie and Crosse on the committee. While Gibson remained a judge, the other three were replaced by John Smith, merchant, W. Richardson and John Pettingell. [10] It proved to be the swan song of the Institution for the Promotion of the Fine Arts and it is probably no coincidence that this was also the year in which Dr. Alderson died, not long after laying the foundation stone of a new building for the Mechanics Institute.

New public rooms opened in 1830 at the corner of Jarratt Street and Kingston Square, later converted into what is now the New Theatre.

Clearly the artists themselves were not willing or able to maintain the Hull and East Riding Institution and the gentlemen who had originally promoted it channelled their energies into the Literary and Philosophical Society and the Mechanics Institutue. [11] W. H. Dikes was for many years curator of the museum of the Literary and Philosophical Society.

The Mechanics Institute seems to have taken as one of its roles the provision of a school of art. Thomas Wilkinson Wallis, the noted wood carver, [12] joined the

Institute as a young man to gain access to its extensive library and attend the drawing classes. The latter were no doubt conducted on the lines established at the Royal Academy and Wallis refers to the removal of the collection of plaster casts to new premises in 1842. [13] On one occasion a lecture was given by Benjamin Robert Haydon, a history painter, probably now best remembered for his quarrels with the Royal Academy and his fellow artists; Wallis remarks that 'He was great on anatomy'.

Haydon remarks in his diary for 3rd May, 1839, "I never witnessed more enthusiasm anywhere than at Hull, the last night. The people are slow but feel deeply. A School of Design was begun, and I do not doubt its complete establishment." It is clear that this was the origin of the School of Art established in 1861.

John Ward was one of the subscribing members and to raise money for the Mechanics Institute a panorama in eight sections of the 'Siege of Hull in 1643' was painted on 3000 square feet of canvas. Unfortunately the artists are not recorded but the project was apparently masterminded by Thomas Earle. [14] The panorama was no doubt decided upon as a work which would have wide popular appeal and be accessible to all in a way in which the formal exhibitions in the Assembly Rooms with their expensive admission fee was not. [15]

There were intermittent exhibitions throughout the century but most of these included, or were dominated by, a miscellany of antiquities or quantities of commercial and industrial artefacts in the show. They were as often as not designed to raise funds for some specific cause such as the infirmary or the lifeboat institution.

A School of Art was formed in 1861 and it was established on a firmer footing in 1878 when it became associated with the Hull Literary and Philosophical Society. A house (number 2) in Albion Street, was purchased for its use and opened on the 1st October. To advertise the event a loan exhibition was staged at the Royal Institution, beginning a week later on 8th October, 1878. This included a large collection of art objects from the South Kensington Museum, a number of oil paintings lent by the Prince of Wales, and local patrons

as well as a miscellany of china, rare autographs, engravings, antique coins and curiosities. Open from 10am till 5pm day tickets were one shilling for the first week, sixpence subsequently; season tickets for members of the society and students for two shillings and sixpence, five shillings for all others; catalogues were sixpence each. The exhibition was opened with an inaugural address given by Dr. A. K. Rollit, president of the Literary and Philosophical Society.

The text which follows will summarise the progress of marine painting in Hull from the end of the eighteenth century to the present. Its development moved in step with the expansion of the port and the construction of the new system of enclosed docks. Until 1778 when the first dock was opened for traffic the only landing place was at the entrance to the river Hull, known as the 'Old Harbour'. The new docks not only represented an expansion of trade and increase in prosperity but a restructuring of the town plan. Since the fourteenth century Hull had been confined within a defensive wall and ditch but these were completely replaced by the Town Docks system, completed in 1829 with the opening of the Junction Dock. A series of new streets were laid down with the first dock and the fine new houses lining Charlotte Street and North Street became the residences of the great merchants who left their former houses in High Street. In their previous location each had a private wharf at the rear so their cargoes could be loaded and unloaded directly supervised by the proprietor. These premises were now left as counting houses in the hands of their clerks.

Artists were attracted into Hull at this exciting and prosperous time to paint the portraits of the merchants and gentry as well as provide them with landscapes and studies of their houses and animals. The activities of the most important of these are described as also the occasional marine artist from outside the region who undertook a commission in Hull. The strength of the local talent is indicated however by the small numbers of the latter. None of these men stayed in Hull for any length of time and certainly did not settle here. In contrast the desire for good quality portraits evidently could not be satisfied by the local artists and John Russell RA had several long periods in the city and eventually died whilst engaged here and is buried in Holy Trinity Church. Sir George Chalmers, the Scottish portrait painter, also worked for the local merchant families as well as painting a portrait of George 3 for the Hull Trinity House.

Until the latter half of the nineteenth century it is also true that none of the local marine painters ever left their home towns to reside in London or any of the other major ports. There were evidently enough patrons who were satisfied with the work of Willoughby, Ward *et al*, to provide a regular living. As the century progressed more and more clients of smaller means were seeking ship portraits and numbers of lesser painters were able to supply the need much as the photographer was later to do. Many of these are firmly in the category of pier-head painters, individuals who would frequent the quaysides touting for business while a ship was loaded or unloaded. Such painters would frequently execute pictures of the river craft and coasting vessels rather than the major sea-going ships which were usually the main subject of the major artists.

Reuben Chappell [16] of Goole has provided us with an invaluable record of the Humber keels and sloops and in this century Joseph Arnold captured on paper many of the trawlers of the North Sea box fleet. Their work, albeit attactive and of considerable historical interest, inevitably tends to be stereotyped; the pier-head artists worked to a formula so as to ensure a picture could be completed quickly and sold cheaply.

While there was a strong demand for ship portraits within the confines of the Humber there was no real temptation to seek fame and fortune elsewhere. From the middle of the nineteenth century however there was a broadening clientele wanting sea-pieces of a more decorative nature, rather than a specific record of a particular ship. William Frederick Settle the sometime pupil and assistant of John Ward took this opportunity to leave Hull and reside in the metropolis though initially retaining his links with the city and with the Royal Yorkshire Yacht Club whose offical artist he was. Sadly his talents as a painter in oils were not appreciated and he never achieved any great reputation in London.

Thomas Somerscales only really developed his art while living abroad in Chile and he was able to return to England a fully fledged marine painter whose work was regularly exhibited at the Royal Academy until his death in 1927. He was widely esteemed in his lifetime and his immense ability both as a landscape artist and a marine painter is again being recognised. The tradition of marine painting still continues in our region and embraces a wide range of talent and diversity of expression.

There are a number of part-time artists supplying pictures of vessels, especially trawlers for retired seamen and fishermen and their families as a remembrance of the recent past. There are also a handful of full-time artists some at the very top of their profession, who regularly exhibit in London and in major shows in Europe and America. The ease of modern transport and communications makes it unnecessary for any talented artist to leave his home territory and settle in the capital. Steven Dews and Colin Verity continue to live and work in East Yorkshire, and have an international reputation receiving important commissions from clients across the world.

THE ORIGINS AND PROGRESS OF MARINE PAINTING IN HULL

Painting in the eighteenth and much of the nineteenth century was still essentially a craft learned by serving an apprenticeship with a master. This was followed by a period as a journeyman, either with the same master or in another workshop to gain a wider experience. Only then could an enterprising young man contemplate establishing his own business. Until the latter half of the nineteenth century the chief function of the marine painter was to provide ship portraits, accurate visual records of particular craft, correct in all their nautical detail, to the satisfaction of their builders, owners or the men who sailed them.

The early marine painters invariably came from the ranks of the house and ship painters whose main occupation was decorating the interior and exterior of shops and houses and applying the paint mop to ships' timbers. Sign-writing and sign-painting was usually part of the trade of these men and it was surely orders for tavern signs coupled with their close contact with shipowners and shipmasters which led the more adept into the art of marine painting. To a man accustomed to wielding the big brush intended to cover the greatest area of timber in the shortest possible time, a sign would give the opportunity of working on a scale more familiar to the artist with his canvas. Vessels of all kinds would be a frequent subject for inn signs in a large port like Hull and it is but a small step from painting sign boards to accepting a commission from a shipowner or mariner for a picture of a favourite ship (fig. 1). There is an inn sign ('The Ship Inn, Home Brew'd beer by Thomas

*1. The Alabama tavern c.1880 at the corner of Chariot Street and Carr Lane, Hull. Over the doorway is a canvas sign of the battle between the **Alabama** and **Kearsage** off Cherbourg in 1864. (Town Docks Museum).*

2. An early oil painting by John Ward of a river scene in the manner of William Anderson (4$^1/_2$ x 6$^3/_4$ in.). (Ferens Art Gallery).

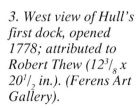

3. West view of Hull's first dock, opened 1778; attributed to Robert Thew (12$^3/_8$ x 20$^1/_2$ in.). (Ferens Art Gallery).

13

*4. The ship **Mayflower** off Hull, 1780 (36 x 51 in.). (Hull Trinity House).*

*5. HMS **Hector** after launching from Blaydes yard, Hessle Cliff, 1743; anonymous artist (27 x 45 in.). (Town Docks Museum).*

Cookman') in the Salisbury Museum dating from c.1820 which would not look out of place framed and hung on the wall.

In the days before street numbering was prevalent painted signs were used by an abundance of shopkeepers, tradesmen and craftsmen to locate and advertise their premises. Occasionally a larger opportunity was given to the artisan to demonstrate his artistic talent. A drawing by George Vertue, dated 1711, of the old headquarters of the East India Company in Leadenhall Street, London, shows a huge pediment painted with sailing ships demonstrating its trading activities across the oceans of the world. We know also that Peter Monamy (1687-1769), who was apprenticed to a house and ship painter in London and who was later a freeman of the Painters Stainers company, furnished a sign for the Portobello Inn with a representation of Admiral Vernon's ('Old Grog') flagship. He was also responsible for decorating the carriage of the ill-fated Admiral Byng with ships and naval trophies. [17] Monamy, inspired by the Van de Veldes who painted so many fine sea pictures for their patron Charles II, provides the link between them and painters such as Thomas Luny (1759-1837) and William Anderson (1757-1837), in the evolution of the native tradition of marine art. Some also like Nicholas Pocock and George Chambers had been seamen or like Robert Cleveley had worked in a shipyard all of which gave them direct practical knowledge of ships and the sea.

Marine painting has two basic strands, on the one hand ship-portrait painting which includes the faithfully reportage of sea battles and naval events, and on the other hand the painting of seascapes in which ships form merely a part of a composition in which the sea in all its moods and elements of the shoreline are equally important. In other words seascapes are the water equivalent of landscape painting. Individual painters might produce works of both types and often the division is blurred when a portrait of a particular vessel is placed in a well realised setting so that the picture can

15

be appreciated as much for its general atmosphere and balanced composition as for any factual record it makes.

In eighteenth century Hull Julius Caesar Ibbetson (1759-1817) is a key figure in the complicated web of relationships among the fraternity of painters. [18] He served a five year apprenticeship with John Fletcher, house and ship painter of Hull, before eventually establishing himself as a landscape artist of repute. In London he was a friend and neighbour of the Scottish marine artist William Anderson, the artist whose work was to make such an impression on Hull's John Ward in his early years (fig. 2). Anderson's pictures belong to the seascape tradition and Ward produced a number of fine river scenes of ships on the Humber, mainly painted on panel, which continued in that vein. Ibbetson was also a friend of Benjamin Gale (1741-1832), originally from Aislaby near Whitby but who was active in Hull for many years as a portrait painter, topographical artist and engraver. [19] Gale became a resident drawing master at Scawby Hall (Lincs.) home of the Nelthorpe family who subscribed to some of Ibbetsons etchings in 1806. This same family were also patrons of George Stubbs, the portrait artist and horse painter, who made a portrait of Sir Henry Nelthorpe, c.1746, Sir John as a boy, c.1756 and again as a young man in 1776. Stubbs came to Hull from York in 1751 and was active in the area for two years and then after his return from Italy he occupied himself with the famous dissections of horses on the Horkstow estate, near South Ferriby (Lincs.) 1756-8. [20]

Evidence of Ibbetson's continuing contact with Hull is the claim made by John Willoughby, portrait and landscape painter, and son of Robert Willoughby, marine painter, to have received instruction from him.

John Raphael Smith painted a portrait of Ibbetson and both men were friendly with George Morland the sporting painter. In 1803 Smith executed a mezzotint engraving of George Wallis, the Hull gunsmith and antiquary. [21] Issued as a commemorative portrait it was prepared under the patronage of the Duke of Clarence, the future William IV, and available by subscription. Born in Derby in 1752 Smith was resident in Yorkshire during the latter years of his life and died in Doncaster, not Worcester as many authorities state, in 1812. An important apprentice of Smith was the notable water-colourist Peter de Wint. From an earlier generation it is worth noting that William Kent (1685-1748) architect, interior designer and painter, born at Bridlington, was apprenticed to a Hull coach painter and house painter but he moved on to London without completing his term. [22]

Hull was a thriving and expanding port at the turn of the century and as we have seen was able to attract many of the fashionable painters of the day such as Stubbs and Smith. Sir George Chalmers (died in London 1791) the Scottish portrait painter produced a splendid full-length study of George III for the Hull Trinity House, in 1775, and excellent portraits of Joseph Outram, wine merchant and mayor, in 1776, and Joseph Sykes another Hull merchant, in 1779. The Outram painting was evidently made to commemorate his laying of the foundation stone of Hulls first enclosed dock in 1775. [23] This was opened to shipping three years later and is shown to great effect in the pair of engravings issued in 1786 by Francis Jukes after original studies by Robert Thew (fig. 3 and pl. 2). Born in Patrington in 1759 the son of a publican he was eventually to be appointed historical engraver to the Prince of Wales and died at Roxley, near Letchworth, Hants. in 1802. [24] The two dock views are the only marine subjects that Thew issued and a pair of oils now in the Ferens Art Gallery though unsigned are considered to be the basis of the engravings though no other paintings have been attributed to his hand and they may well have been copied from the prints. The 'West View' shows in minute detail a great array of ships including the *Molly* and *Manchester* of the Hull whaling fleet; the latter was the first to enter the dock and the venue for a grand celebration dinner. A very accomplished pair of oval canvases, dated 1780 but unsigned, hang in the Hull Trinity House (fig. 4). One shows two vessels at the entrance to the 'old Harbour' with the citadel in the background and the other the ship *Mayflower* off the Hull waterfront. The style shows some affinities to the

6. *The shipyard at Hessle Cliff, painted by J. W. Carmichael, signed and dated 1829 (34 x 47$^1/_4$ in.). (Ferens Art Gallery).*

7. An armed whaleship (26 x 38 in.); Robert Willoughby, c.1810. (Town Docks Museum).

8. *The buoy yacht* **Zephyr** *of the Hull Trinity House, off the Hull waterfront (19 x 37 in.); John Ward c.1835. (Ferens Art Gallery).*

work of Robert Willoughby but the identity of the artist remains uncertain. [25] They might be the work of Thomas Fletcher but there is only one canvas certainly by his hand to which they can be compared.

The earliest dateable painting of a *named* vessel on the Humber is the anonymous canvas of HMS *Hector* launched by Hugh Blaydes at Hessle Cliffs in 1743. [26] As it is not signed it is impossible to say whether this was executed by an artist based in the region or someone who perhaps was employed through the auspices of the Admiralty (fig. 5 and pl. 1).

In the Town Docks Museum there are two canvases depicting the whaling fleet of Sir Samuel Standidge in 1769 (pl. 3) and 1788 respectively. The former is in fact copied, with little alteration, except that it is reversed, from the engraving made by Boydell after the painting by Charles Brooking (1723-59) of the 'Greenland Whale Fishery' which now hangs at Greenwich. The 1788 piece depicts the *Mary*, *Samuel*, and *Lady Jane* and is evidently an authentic representation of these vessels

by the same but anonymous hand. Clearly the Standidge fleet of 1769, purportedly illustrating the *Berry*, *Britannia* and *British Queen*, was painted long after these ships had ceased sailing, as a companion to the 1788 canvas to grace the walls of the Standidge home and counting house in High Street.

To further demonstrate the vigorous artistic activity in the city we may also note that John Russell (1744-1806) the well-known portrait painter (in pastels and oils) came to Hull to fulfil a number of commissions in connection with the Hull Subscription Library. Founded in 1775 by Thomas Lee (died 1779), of the firm of Paed, Lee and Co., soapmakers, it was for many years the intellectual hub of the city. Russell painted portraits of Lee, Dr. Henry Moyes (1750-1807) and Dr. George Birkbeck (1776-1861). Moyes though blind had a great ability as a scientific lecturer which he displayed at the library in 1802. Birkbeck, born in Settle, was the founder of the Mechanics Institutue movement and gave a course in 'mechanical philosophy' to subscrib-

9. One of two surviving mahogany panels from the stateroom of the paddle steamer **Waterwitch** *($6^1/_2$ x 12 in.); Edward Duncan, 1833. (Private Collection).*

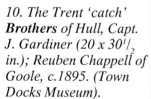

10. The Trent 'catch' **Brothers** *of Hull, Capt. J. Gardiner (20 x $30^1/_2$ in.); Reuben Chappell of Goole, c.1895. (Town Docks Museum).*

*11. The S.S. **Romeo** of the Wilson Line (20 x 33 in.); R. D. Widdas, 1882. (Town Docks Museum).*

*12. The steam trawler **Filey** (H.8) of the Hull Steam Fishing and Ice Co.; Joseph Arnold, 1914. (Town Docks Museum).*

*13. HMS **Clio,** aboard which the artist served from 1863 (14 x 20 in.); Thomas Jacques Somerscales, 1923. (Ferens Art Gallery).*

14. Lithographic poster; Harry Hudson Rodmell, 1921. (Town Docks Museum).

ers in 1805. This portrait was a gift to the subscription library from the artist and in acknowledgement Russell was made an honorary member shortly before his death in Hull in 1806. [27] He was buried in Holy Trinity Church where a memorial slab can still be seen on the pavement of the south choir aisle. William Beilby the celebrated glass enameller of Newcastle also came to the city, after residing in Scotland for a number of years, and in 1814 advertised himself as a drawing master. He died aged 81 in 1819 at his residence in English Street near the Humber Bank. Thomas Bewick was apprenticed to Ralph Beilby, William's brother and later became his partner before taking over the firm in the name of Thomas Bewick and Son. [28] The workshop supplied a variety of blocks to local printers such as Ferraby and Peck and on 19 December 1787 supplied a wood cut for the title decoration (mast head) of the *Hull Packet* which was used for the first time in the first issue published in the new year. This shows an allegorical figure supporting the city arms with a view of the entrance to the river Hull and the citadel.

There is no evidence of ship-painting on glass in Britain but a considerable volume of such works were produced in France, Germany and particularly Flanders. The technique was to paint on the under-surface of the glass so the artist had to work out his design in reverse which accounts for a number of errors and anomalies, especially the lettering of the inscriptions and the letters and numbers which might appear on the vessel's sails. The earliest ship portrait on glass dates from 1805 executed by Wenzelaus Wieden of Ostend and he was followed by Petrus Weyts (1799-1855) the most prolific of the glass painters who with his two sons moved from Ostend and based himself at Antwerp from c.1838.

Thomas Whitcombe (c.1752-1824) an important London-based marine painter visited here as is indicated by the portrait of the *North Briton* acquired by John Ward which depicts the Hull whaler of that name, active in the fleet 1805 to 1830. [29] John Wilson Carmichael (1799-1868) of Newcastle produced a handsome painting of the 'Shipyard at Hessle Cliffs'

dated 1829 (fig. 6 and pl. 6). George Chambers (1803-40) of Whitby and London and visited the town two years earlier to paint the brig *Spartan* (pl. 5), and there is a watercolour of the Old Harbour signed and dated 1834 in the Ferens Art Gallery. [30] There is no documentary record of their presence in Hull and we do not know what direct contact they may have had with the resident artists. It is noteworthy however that a watercolour in the Laing Art Gallery by Carmichael of the *Dandie Dinmont* (built at Shields in 1848) is a direct copy of John Ward's lithograph of this subject.

According to Benjamin Brooks, but not verified by any other source, another eminent visitor was the portrait artist Benjamin West RA (1738-1820; president of the Royal Academy in 1792) who whilst in Hull lived on the first floor premises occupied by T. Brooks, carver and gilder in Blackfriargate until 1825. A drawing by West of the shop with its gilt lead sign of the Golden Boy is reproduced in the *Hull News* supplement, 1897, accompanying an autobiographical note by Benjamin Brooks (the son of Thomas Brooks) who established himself in London as a notable print seller and publisher. Before moving south Benjamin claimed to have 'the entire work of Sir Clifford and Lady Constable and decorated the drawing room of Burton Constable .... We had the patronage of J. R. Pease, John Barkworth Snr., Dr. Chalmers, Dr. Alderson, Sir Tatton Sykes, Henry Broadley, John Malam, Joseph Gee. When a boy, my mother took me in a sedan chair to a ball at Mr. Wilson's home in Salthouse Lane'. The latter was of course the founder of the firm of Thomas Wilson and Sons, the eminent shipowners.

Hull evidently attracted artists and painters of all kinds who were seeking to obtain work from the thriving mercantile community as well as the landed gentry on both sides of the Humber. It was also a custom of the period to send on tour small groups of paintings, or even individual canvases if the subject was striking enough, either because they were by celebrated artists or depicted newsworthy occurrences or famous historic events which were likely to be a public draw. In June 1800 two works by the landscape and history painter Phillipe

Jacques de Loutherbourg (1740-1812) were exhibited at the Cross Keys Hotel, Market Place. [31] At the cost of a one shilling admission fee the public could see 'The Great Attack on Valenciennes at Sunset' and the 'Victory of Lord Howe on the first of June'. This latter painting recording the notable naval victory of 1794 is now in the National Maritime Museum at Greenwich and Loutherbourg painted a great many maritime set pieces of battles and of dramatic shipwrecks and storm scenes.

The short-lived Hull and East Riding Institution for the Promotion of the Fine Arts, founded in February 1827 staged Hull's first major art exhibition in the same year. Pictures were submitted by local artists and collectors, a handful of artists from York and Leeds were included and a considerable representation from the metropolis. The works included portraits, landscapes, genre studies and marines by Phineas Lowther, T. F. Wilson, Thomas Binks, William Anderson, C. M. Powell, John Willoughby, John Varley, John Ward, J. B. Crome, George Arnald ARA, William Etty ARA, A. W. Calcott RA, James Ward ARA and many other lesser names. At least two of the judges, C. R. Alderson and Edward Gibson were amateur artists the former being a physician and the son of Dr. John Alderson (1758-1829) and elder brother of Dr. James Alderson. Christopher Richard Alderson (whose cousin Amelia married John Opie the portrait painter) provided a number of illustrations for his brother's description of the sperm whale stranded on the Holderness coast in 1825 which was subsequently mounted in the grounds of Burton Constable Hall. [32] The Institution was apparently dissolved soon after 1829 without its supporters being able to realise their ambition of establishing a gallery for the permanent display of works of art to the citizens of Hull. Edward Gibson, (1787-1859) shipbuilder and shipowner, mayor of Hull in 1834 and 1835 and one of the Institution's supporter's, is known to have painted a number of watercolours and there is a somewhat diagrammatic drawing signed by him of the Hull whalers beset in Davis Straits in 1830 (see directory). Whether he was actually on board one of the vessels or prepared the painting from someone's eye-witness description is not clear.

In 1835 he was the chairman of the organising committee of the 'Exhibition of the Fine Arts' which was staged in the rooms of the school of medicine in Kingston Square. Profits from the proceeds of admission were to be given to the infirmary and medical charities, though with a family season ticket costing 10 shillings and single season ticket 5s. the patrons must have been decidedly few in number and restricted to the more comfortably off members of the community.

The increasing success of the whaling fleet seems to have made a particular impact on the development of marine painting in Hull and almost all of the earliest marine canvases of local provenance, by Thomas Fletcher and Robert Willoughby, depict vessels engaged in the Arctic whaling trade. It is perhaps not surprising that the adventure and excitement of hunting the great leviathans of the deep in the far northern regions persuaded ship-owners and mariners that it was worth making some permanent record of the vessels involved. The often high financial return, which was the rule until the third decade of the nineteenth century when several disasters befell the fleet, also provided the money to make frequent commissions for such pictures. Willoughby remains active into the 1830's though his later work seems to be mainly portraiture and no ship portraits have been identified later than 1817 (fig. 7). As he bowed out Binks and Griffin established themselves as two of the most popular painters of the period though Willoughby died as late as 1843 not far short of the middle of the century and only six years before John Ward. Despite the wide range of influences which the local marine painters could have been exposed to, they seem to have remained largely self-contained, they were vying with, and occasionally borrowing from, one another within the confines of the city rather than with their contemporaries or immediate predecessors active outside of Hull. Ward is the exception with his obvious debt to Anderson but this is really only apparent in his small seascapes on panel. His full scale ship portraits with their usually very adroit views of the waterfront contain no obvious features or tricks of style taken from the work of the big names of British marine art based in London or elsewhere (fig. 8). Equally, despite regularly exhibiting his work in London between 1831 and 1841, Ward gained no great following though the work of Robert Strickland Thomas RN, a part-time painter and ex-naval officer clearly borrows from Ward's naval subjects which feature in his lithographs and his outstanding Academy piece of HMS *Britannia* painted in 1847.

John Ward undoubtedly outshines all other local marine painters and can be numbered amongst the best in nineteenth century Britain, indeed in Europe. Apprenticed to Thomas Meggitt but influenced by the work of Robert Willoughby he was trained as a house painter, a trade which he pursued until the 1830s. His earliest dateable work is from 1821 which suggests that he went through the normal seven years term with his master and was only able to devote significant time and effort to marine painting after his apprenticeship was completed at the age of twenty-one or thereabouts. In his maturity he attempted to distil the accummulated knowledge of ship types and make a lithographic record of all kinds of vessels in a variety of rigs. These prints were intended to be compiled into a manual of instruction for marine painters but sadly his premature death at the age of forty-nine prevented the project being completed.

One of the London painters who established Hull contacts was W. J. Huggins who in 1836 provided a series of pictures to decorate the saloon of the P.S. *Vivid* with coastal views. [33] This was shortly after he was appointed marine painter to William IV and was probably chosen because he was fashionable rather than because of the superiority of his work over the local artists, and indeed the bulk of his work is decidedly mediocre. The *Vivid* was however launched as one of the crack steamers of the Hull Steam Packet Co. for the highly competitive Hull-London trade and to choose a 'big name' like Huggins to be involved in its decoration was obviously an extra selling point.

Huggins also painted a picture of the *Vivid* which was engraved by Rosenberg. Two panels, of a steamer in heavy seas and off Spurn, signed by Edward Duncan,

Huggins son-in-law, come from the stateroom of the *Waterwitch*, a sister ship of the *Vivid*. Huggins, his son and Duncan all exhibited examples of their work in Hull in 1835 (fig. 9). In 1837 T. Brooks and Son, carvers and gilders, undertook the fitting out of the saloon of the P.S. *Victoria* belonging to the rival Humber Union Steam Packet Co. thought no mention is made of the inclusion of pictures of any kind in the decor. [34]

Ship portrait painting after Ward moved decidedly down market and was largely left to competent but uninspiring artists like W. D. Penny though the watercolours of S. H. Wilson are always skilfully drawn often with considerable dramatic flair.

It is only in the second half of the nineteenth century that painters like W. F. Settle and Henry Redmore were able to devote themselves exclusively to the art of canvas painting and the involvement with the trade of house and ship painting was finally abandoned. This state of affairs demonstrates the growing ability of the artist to find sufficient purchasers for his work so as to make a living solely as a marine artist. There was an increasing number of people with the time and inclination to interest themselves in marine painting (indeed fine art generally), other than just the shipowners and shipmasters who had hitherto been the main stimulus to the art.

In the early days the pieces purchased were ship portraits, accurate reproductions of particular craft made to specific order by someone with a special interest in that vessel. The canvases or panels often depicted the ship on an empty ocean, a buoy, small boat or fragment of floating wreckage being the only subsidiary items, with little or no attempt to provide a setting. John Ward was however outstanding in his ability to provide an attractive composition incorporating the Hull waterfront or an arctic landscape in addition to an accurate but vital portrayal of a particular vessel, enlivened with very effective staffage.

After the middle of the century there was a broadening clientele for sea pieces, outside the fraternity of merchants, shipowners and sea captains, made up of individuals who wanted canvases simply to decorate their homes. Redmore was the local artists who was especially able to respond to the Victorian romanticism which delighted in storms and wrecks. He executed some ship portraits but was largely kept busy producing seascapes often on a large scale. These helped satisfy a burgeoning middle class which created a demand for all kinds of pictures, conversation pieces, portraits and genre pieces to fill their walls, to a large degree as an expression of status and their position on the social ladder.

Even the shipowners were often acquiring romantic sea pieces and storm scenes though presumably for their houses, since a picture of a vessel in distress is hardly suitable for a shipping office and is not going to inspire potential customers with confidence! Gone were the days when an owner could hope to have a picture of practically every vessel he had ever bought. By his death in 1869 Thomas Wilson had been the proud possessor of nearly sixty ships which swelled to a staggering ninety nine when his company acquired Bailey and Leetham his major rival in 1903. Clearly only a select few of the finest and most prestigious components of the fleet would be selected for recording on canvas. The Wilson Line commissioned a painting of the *Hindoo*, crack steamer on the Calcutta route, from the Liverpool artist Samuel Walters and most of the large and powerful steamers built for the transatlantic route were painted by Antonio Jacobsen (1850-1921) the New York ship portrait painter. [35] The larger companies had a world-wide trade and this more cosmopolitan outlook often meant that they ordered pictures from artists outside their home port, though the Wilson Line did also order a whole series of large watercolour drawings by the Hull artist S. H. Wilson who himself seems to have been peripatetic and is known to have painted vessels in Chester and London. Another reason why fewer pictures were being ordered for the boardroom and office was the increasing popularity of ship models which provided a detailed three-dimensional record of the ship and its fittings far beyond what the most detailed drawing or picture could do. Perhaps the abiding image of a visit to the headquarters of any of the great shipping offices from the late nineteenth century down to the present is of committee rooms and corridors filled with large-scale models in grand cases beautifully turned and finished. Up to the beginning of this century when professional model makers, both individuals and companies, began to provide this service, most of these splendid pieces were produced in the carpenters shop of the yard which built the full-sized ship.

The overwhelming majority of ship portraits produced in the second half of the last century were painted at the request of the captain or a member of the crew. Practically every ships officer in those days must have acquired at some time in his career at least one such piece of a vessel he had a particular association with. Many of the painters producing these works were trained like their predecessors in the house and ship painting tradition but increasingly we see the appearance of the 'pier-head' painter. This was a man who often literally sat on the quayside waiting for vessels to dock and then offering his services to the officers and crews as they came ashore. These individuals were often ex-mariners, largely self-taught though in some cases they might have had some simple training in draughtsmanship. They painted very quickly, often in watercolour, though certainly not eschewing oils, producing simple stereotyped compositions. The classic example of the pier-head painter from the Humber region was Reuben Chappell (1870-1940) son of a Goole joiner and cabinet maker. His first job was with a local photographer and the frequent task of tinting photographic prints led him on to painting. He charged five shillings for a watercolour and thirty shillings for an oil and in his long career is estimated to have completed over 12,000 pictures. [36] (fig. 10)

The artist chosen by the mariner to provide his ship portrait was not necessarily in his home port or even in England. Throughout Europe there were artists producing colourful and simple but usually well-drawn, studies of sailing ships and steamers. Amsterdam, Copenhagen, Marseilles, Genoa, Livorno, Venice and Naples are frequent sources of ship portraits. An important influence on the development of marine painting in the Mediterannean was the custom of presenting votive work to hang in the local church. These represent the way in which an individual was rescued from death and serious injury by the supposed intervention of the Virgin Mary or a patron saint. In the ports of the Mediterannean shore many of these pictures would inevitably be concerned with mariners and travellers by sea thus helping to foster a tradition of ship-painting. A remarkable collection of pictures of all kinds of incidents, the earliest dating from about 1800 is preserved in the church of Our Lady of Montenero which stands on a hill overlooking Livorno in Tuscany.

Antwerp can be singled out as the home of the Weyts family who specialised in painting on glass and despite the difficulties of working in reverse on the back of the glass sheet, these must have sold quite cheaply. The Town Docks Museum has two such pieces of schooners, humble craft belonging to small-scale ship owners, bearing the names of Goole master mariners. There were also Chinese artists working in Hong Kong and Shanghai and others who had set up shop in India; Lai Fong of Canton for example was working in Calcutta where he advertised himself as ship and portrait painter, tobacconist and commission agent.

The pier-head artist working quickly and for a low return was able for many years to fend off competition from his potential rival the photographer. Indeed as we have seen Chappell was actually inspired to paint after being employed in a photographers's studio. R. D. Widdas (1826-85) was a portrait and animal painter and in his early career a photographer too. He was essentially a jobbing painter but painted at least three marines including one of the whaler *Diana* beset in the ice and another a large panoramic canvas entitled 'Shipping on the Humber' on which is depicted all the principal types of vessel which might be seen visiting Hull in 1879, everything from a fishing smack to a Wilson steamer in the Scandinavian trade (fig. 11).

It was not until c.1900 that we see the appearance, at least in Hull, of the specialist marine photographer and for the next quarter of century Marcus Barnard made his living selling his postcard pictures from various addresses around the town. For much of this period however there was still one very active ship-portrait painter in the port, this was Joseph Arnold, Hull's nearest equivalent to Reuben Chappell. Apparently an ex-fisherman he was prolific in his gouache studies of local trawlers, many of them belonging to the North Sea box fleet, which he sold to the owners, skippers and crew (fig. 12).

Hull's greatest marine painter of the late nineteenth century was Thomas Jacques Somerscales (1842-1927); the son of a master mariner he only started painting seriously when working as a schoolmaster in Chile and didn't come back to Hull until 1892 so his skill developed quite independently of the local tradition (fig. 13). He exhibited every year at the Royal Academy from the year of his return until his death in 1927. Most of his canvases display a love of the open sea and great sailing ships but he did paint actual historical events such as shipwrecks and naval engagements. It was his painting of ships of the Chilean navy which helped to establish his reputation in South America and back in England he painted 'The sinking of th *Scharnhorst* off the Falklands Islands, 1914'. There are also a few straightforward ship portraits including a study of the S.S. *Immingham* of the Great Central Railway which is in the Town Docks Museum (pl. 43).

The larger sea ports of Britain and many of the smaller ones such as Scarborough, Kings Lynn and Great Yarmouth were for many years nurseries for home-grown talent, painters of ships and the sea mostly brought up as house and ship painters but later followed by a miscellany of retired seamen and self-taught artists. An increasing demand for elaborate seascapes could not always be met by the local painters who might not be up to picture-making in a manner requiring the skills more often found in the studio of one of the major artists living in the metropolis. Redmore in Hull fulfilled the popular demand for some thirty years but no-one followed directly in his footsteps. Somerscales however was accorded the sort of national recognition none of his predecessors in Hull had ever achieved. He was able to work in his home town and receive commissions from all over the country as well as making regular trips back to Chile where to this day he is virtually regarded as the country's national artist.

After the end of the 1914-18 war the demands of the advertising industry provided employment for a great number of talented artists. The boom in ocean travel and the expansion of the great liner companies led to the creation of some of the finest poster art ever produced. Harry Hudson Rodmell, who was born in Hull but spent his working life as an artist in Hornsea, was a highly successful designer of such posters and throughout the 1920's and 1930's; he maintained a large output of graphic work, a considerable sample of which is preserved in the Town Docks Museum (fig. 14).

It is good that a new generation of local marine painters is active and three names figure prominently amongst the exponents of the art namely, J. Steven Dews, Colin Verity and David Bell, (pls. 52-9), all of whom have reputations extending well beyond the confines of the city. The ship portrait is an essential part of the output of all three though many of the vessels they paint are now long gone. Often the picture is an historical reconstruction purchased by the individual ship lover or company wanting a record of a sailing ship or steamer of a vanished age. Colin Verity does however keep a close association with Ben Line producing works which enhance their offices or which may be used in their annual calendar. Steven Dews has painted for Amoco a series of historic vessels, from the *Golden Hind* to Naomi James yacht *Express Crusader*, and has recently painted a number of studies of the yachts which took part in the Americas cup series in Australia.

So long as there are ships afloat on the sea there will be marine painters to capture them on canvas. The number of shipping companies has however much diminished and though Hull's great tradition of marine painting, stretching back over two hundred years, may still continue to inspire future generations these artists will be satisfying patrons mostly outside the port of Hull and often in countries overseas.

THOMAS FLETCHER AND HIS KINSMEN

The earliest ship portrait which can certainly be ascribed to the hand of a Hull artist is a canvas of the Hull whaleships 'Molly and Friends' signed 'T. Fletcher pinxt'.[37] It was commissioned by Angus Sadler, master of the Molly from 1796 to 1802 whose initials AS appear on the string of whaleboats in the foreground. The Arctic whaling trade which developed into a very lucrative business for the Hull merchants and shipowners was very important in the establishment of the local tradition of marine painting. Robert Willoughby who represents the next generation was quite prolific and whaling vessels figure prominently amongst his subjects (fig. 15 and pl. 8). He was followed by John Ward who painted some of the very finest scenes of Arctic whaling, unsurpassed by any other contemporary in Britain or elsewhere.

The 'Molly and Friends', which hangs in the Town Docks Museum is the *only* picture which can so far be attributed to Thomas Fletcher but his skill in the rendition of the ships is such that we can be sure this work is not just a 'one-off' production. On the reverse the canvas is branded with a triangle enclosing the initials TF and the date 1789 is inscribed directly adjacent, though the painting is unlikely to have been executed earlier than 1796 the year in which Sadler was first appointed captain.

Fletcher belonged to a family of house and ship painters and ship chandlers but was the first of these so far as we know to apply himself as a marine artist. A trade card of a John Fletcher (Castle Museum, York) is decorated with examples of his stock, including a sextant, speaking trumpet, sand-glass, compass and

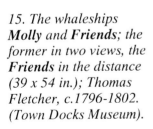

15. The whaleships **Molly** *and* **Friends***; the former in two views, the* **Friends** *in the distance (39 x 54 in.); Thomas Fletcher, c.1796-1802. (Town Docks Museum).*

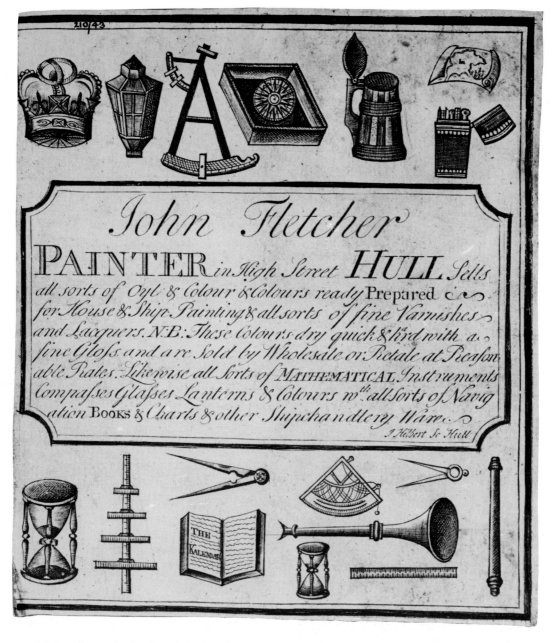

16. Trade card of John Fletcher, engraved by J. Hilbert of Hull. (York Castle Museum).

beer tankard. [38] It was engraved by John Hilbert, active in Hull c.1730-40 who published 'A View of Hull' in 1737 and 'A prospect of Hull Cross' in 1734. [39] The card proclaims Fletcher as the seller of 'all sorts of oyl and colour and colours ready prepared for House and Ship Painting and all sorts of fine Varnishes and Lacquers . . . . Likewise all sorts of Mathematical Instruments, Compasses, glasses, lanterns and colours with all sorts of navigation books and charts and other shipchandlery ware' (fig. 16). He was the son of Christopher Fletcher, a Hessle shipwright, and in 1726 was apprenticed to John Campsall, a carver and compass maker, and a burgess of Hull. Admitted a freeman himself, in 1733 John Fletcher was paid £9 for an altar piece at St. Mary's, Lowgate, in 1752, though whether for carving it or painting it, or both, is not known. [40] John Campsall had himself received £3.1s.0d for carving a 'ffount top', also for St. Mary's, in 1703.

Julius Caesar Ibbetson (1759-1817) was apprenticed to Fletcher between 1772-7, which makes a term of only five years rather than the usual one of seven. The trade of the ship painter was just that and they set to with large pots and buckets and long handled brushes or mops to paint and varnish ships timbers, within and without. Ibbetson was brought to Hull by his father some seventy miles from Farnley Moor, near Leeds, in response to a newspaper advertisement and was quickly disappointed by the work he was put to 'and he could only practise drawing and other painting, at silent hours - - - He did notwithstanding so far advance in skill as to paint several signs which were very much admired'. [41] Subsequently he was a scene painter with Tate Wilkinson, the actor-manager, whose company of players made an annual tour of Yorkshire theatres from York to Hull, Leeds, Wakefield, Doncaster and Pontefract. [42] Ibbetson was eventually to achieve a considerable reputation as a landscape artist, indeed he is one of the founders of the English tradition which was to reach its finest expression in the work of John Constable.

It is significant that Ibbetson initially found sign-painting to be his only real means of artistic expression.

The demand for signs extended beyond inns and taverns to all kinds of commercial premises which before it became customary to use street numbers were located by a carved figure or a painted board.

Thomas Fletcher was admitted freeman by apprenticeship to John Fletcher 30 April 1747 and from 1777 Thomas was also parish clerk to Holy Trinity Church in which post he was succeeded, by his younger son Rouncival, in 1802 which is probably the year that he died. [43]

Thomas and his wife had at least nine children and it is their eldest son also called Thomas, born 1759 but baptised some two years later on 11 June 1761 whom should probably be identified as the painter of 'The *Molly* and *Friends*' since the father would have been greatly advanced in years at the time of its execution. Young Thomas was also elected the first junior warden of the Rodney Lodge and was a founder member of the Minerva Lodge of Freemasons, established 1782-3, and was worshipful master in 1785, 1788 and 1795. [44] This masonic connection we see repeated later by John Ward who was elected worshipful master of the Humber Lodge in 1829. Both of these lodges were particularly associated with the maritime fraternity, including shipowners and master mariners, the individuals who were most interested in having a record made of the vessels they owned or navigated.

A receipt dated 7 June 1783 in the archives of Burton Constable hall records the payment of £27. 6. 4½d to 'Thomas Fletcher, painter and colourman' for supplying various paints, pigments and oils.

Thomas married Elizabeth St. Quintin on the 6 January 1794 at Holy Trinity Church and his name appears in Hull's first trade directory as a painter in High Street. Thomas Fletcher (Snr.), clerk to Holy Trinity Church was living at Higson Court, Blanket Row in that year. Rouncival (b.1764) was a painter, carver and gilder also in High Street, then at 23 Finkle Street (1803-5) and finally in 12 Castle Street. He married Winefred (sic) Williamson, a Roman Catholic, so it is evidence of a considerable degree of tolerance, some thirty years before the acts of toleration were passed, that he was allowed to follow his father as clerk to Holy Trinity Church, the principal seat of Anglican worship in the city. [45] He died on 29 December 1823 at the age of 59, correctly recorded in the parish register but incorrectly in the *Hull Advertiser* as 57. [46]

His son of the same name was born 22 June 1804 [47] and appears in the trade directories for the first time in 1823 as carver and gilder at 65 Mytongate and at 3 New Dock Wall in 1826. In 1838 Rouncival Fletcher (Jnr.) is described as an artist at 8 Worship Street. John Fletcher (bapt. 1767) youngest brother of Thomas and Rouncival was a carver and gilder at 18 Dagger Lane, 1817-23 and in 1826 at Robinson Row, both addresses one may note close to the Minerva Lodge. A George Fletcher was active as a ship-chandler in High Street until 1803 whereafter his widow Jane continued in business in partnership with Thomas Clarkson and then by herself from c.1817. A Miss Fletcher of 3 New Dock Wall was advertising drawing lessons in 1824, at one guinea per person, three times a week at her home or twice a week at the pupil's house. [48]

ROBERT WILLOUGHBY (1768-1843) AND HIS KINSMEN

As an individual Robert Willoughby is scarcely less shadowy than Thomas Fletcher but a substantial number of canvases bearing his signature have survived. They show a preponderance of whaling ships and indeed he is the principal artist responsible for recording the vessels of the Hull whaling fleet during its heyday in the first half of the nineteenth century. Willoughby's baptismal record has not been discovered but he was apparently born in 1768 the son of John Willoughby (I) whose daughter Sarah was baptised at Holy Trinity Church in 1761 and a son Paul in 1765.

The earliest dated canvas, and most usefully they are frequently both signed and dated, is a magnificent painting of the whaling fleet of Samuel Cooper, one of the principal whaleship owners of Hull. It is an ambitious and striking canvas which measures 55 by 70 in. and shows Willoughby to be a skilled artist at the height of his powers. The four ships, *Thomas, Brothers, Samuel* and *North Briton*, fill the picture, each in two positions, profile and stern view, making an impressive and complicated array of masts and sails. The weakest part of the composition, as in all of his paintings which include details of the Arctic scenery, are the icebergs and floes in the foreground though the figures clambering over them in pursuit of bears and seals are very appealing. It is signed in full on a small clump of ice in the left hand corner, *R Willoughby pinxit et delin. Apl. 1st 1803*, the date resumably being that on which the commission was completed. (fig. 17 and pl. 9)

Samuel Cooper, merchant and shipowner, was born

17. Whaleships of the Cooper fleet; (54 x 71 in.). Robert Willoughby, 1803 (Town Docks Museum).

18. *Savile Street, Hull, Westerdale's yard; note the vessels in the dock behind (24$^1/_2$ x 32$^1/_2$); Robert Willoughby, c.1810. (Ferens Art Gallery).*

19. Westerdales house, 1 Pier Street, with vessels in the Hull roads (24$^1/_2$ x 32$^1/_2$); Robert Willoughby, c.1815. (Hull Museums).

*20. The brig **Henry** (21 x 30 in.); John Willoughby, 1820. (Town Docks Museum).*

21. *Portrait of an unknown master mariner (30 x 25 in.); Robert Willoughby, 1805. (National Maritime Museum, Greenwich).*

in Nottingham in 1775 and had over a period of some forty years an interest in a total of eleven Hull whalers, latterly with his brother William Spyvee Cooper (1783-1841). Samuel's son Henry Cooper MD (1807-91), is rather better known to Hull historians chiefly for his involvement in the campaign to improve living conditions in the city and concern for public health. He was knighted by Queen Victoria at the time of the royal visit of 1854, during his term of office as mayor of Hull.

The painting of the fleet is the earliest of Willoughby's canvases so far identified and since it clearly represents the work of a mature artist this means that his entire output from the end of the previous entury is now missing or languishing unrecognised. [49] This is very much an exceptional production and typically Willoughby painted on a stock canvas of 24 by 36 in. showing an individual vessel in two views, a port side profile and a three quarter view. There may be no additional features though whaleboats or fragmentary ice floes often add a little variety to the scene. Other canvases of merchant vessels include familiar pieces of local topography such as Flamborough Head or Spurn Head and its lighthouses. [50] Willoughby also painted portraits and two studies of female sitters, both unidentified, have been seen, one dated 1817 and the other December 1839.

Also attributed to Willoughby, though unsigned, is a view of Savile Street in 1810 which depicts a group of workmen hauling timbers out of the yard of William Westerdale, mast, block and pump maker (fig. 18) [51] A companion piece shows the front of the workshop with the ship *Wellington* lying in dock immediately alongside. A top-hatted figure welcoming some ladies aboard is probably Westerdale himself. Another important early Hull view by the same hand is a painting of the waterfront as it was soon after the completion of the Humber Dock. The spoil from the excavation was used to extend outwards into the river creating an entirely new frontage which was developed as Nelson Street. This picture was evidently also commissioned by Westerdale since the principal feature is his newly erected house, the first to be built in Pier Street c.1815.

On the left is a Ferris wheel and a hurdy gurdy man surrounded by a crowd of children and a warship and other vessels can be seen anchored in the Hull Roads (fig. 19 and pl. 11). [52]

Willoughby's figures are always naive and awkward and on at least one occasion he employed another artist to paint them for him. Another canvas in the Hull Museum collection shows a crowd of vessels in the Humber whilst a group of fish wives lay out their produce for inspection on the river bank. Adjacent to them is the inscription 'Figures by Brooks', no doubt Thomas Brooks, house and ship carver, gilder, glass and picture frame maker (died 1850 aged 77) uncle (not father as some sources state) of Thomas Brooks (1818-92) portrait and genre painter. The latter trained under Henry Perronet Briggs, RA, nephew of Philothea Perronet Briggs who was married in 1781 to Thomas Thompson, principal in the mercantile house of William Wilberforce. Briggs was cousin of their son Gen. Thomas Perronet Thompson, governor of Sierra Leone. [53]

In January 1807 Willoughby advertises himself as having moved to Savile Street, so he would have been close by Westerdales Yard and all the activity which centred around Hull's first enclosed dock completed in 1778. [54] He still describes himself as a house, ship and sign painter and all the Hull marine painters of the eighteenth century and first half of the nineteenth century remained firmly in the artisan tradition. They were jobbing painters who ran workshops which undertook all the basic tasks of house and ship painting and sign writing as their principal employment. The painting of canvases remained a specialised activity to which the master may have directed much of his time while his journeyman and apprentices carried on the daily routine.

Willoughby demonstrated his versatility when in October 1812 he advertised an exhibition of his experiments in glass-working in miniature 'including a beautiful model ship'. They were shown at the premises of Mr. Wayres, a hatter, in Silver Street for an entry fee of one shilling a head. [55] In November the same year he advised the public that his evening drawing school would re-open at his residence, 8 Castle Row on the 16th of the month starting after the end of the exhibition. [56]

The parish register of Holy Trinity Church records the marriage of Robert Willoughby and Elizabeth Smith on 22 August 1792 and his children were subsequently baptised in the same church. [57] He is last recorded in the 1842 trade directory at 27 Annes Place, Sykes Street and died aged 75 on 22 March 1845. His wife predeceased him in 1826 at the age of 53 at Boston, Lincs., 'Elizabeth wife of Robert Willoughby, artist, late of this place (Hull) and mother of John Willoughby, artist of this town. [58]

The *Hull Advertiser*, for 1 November 1794, indicates that up till then a John Willoughby had been in business in High Street as a house, ship and sign painter, and the trade directory of 1791 lists him at Salthouse Lane, possibly his home address. John announces that he is stepping down in favour of his brother Robert who is presumably the marine painter of that name (b.1768). The latter appears in the Hull directories for the first time in 1803 as a house, ship and sign painter in High Street though the *Hull Advertiser*[59] gives an address 'near the new gaol' when he was advertising for two journeyman to be employed by the year, which implies a thriving workshop with plenty of business.

The John Willoughby who advertises himself in 1823 as 'artist and painter in general' pupil to the late Julius Caesar Ibbetson was probably the son of one or other of the two brothers John and Robert. Transferring from Carr Lane to 7 Waterworks Street, an address listed in the trade directories as an artists repository, he offered 'Portraits in oils at two guineas and upwards, bronzing and gilding and varnishing in all its departments. Every description of drawing materials'. [60]

In 1827 'Mr. John Willoughby, portrait and landscape painter begs leave most respectfully to intimate to his friends and the public in general that he purposes establishing at his residence in Savile Street, an Evening academy for the instruction of pupils in draw-

ing'.[61] Four years later his death is recorded 'Early on Sunday morning at his residence in Savile Street after a short illness, to the inexpressible grief of a large circle of friends to whom he was endeared by amiable disposition and unassuming manners. Mr. John Willoughby in the 37th year of his age. Although carrying on his business as a house painter, Mr. W. had long been distinguished as an artist and many of his performances both in landscape and portrait departments have been greatly admired and excited much attention at the late exhibition of the Hull and East Riding Institution.' [62]

Willoughby showed his work at the first exhibition of the Hull and East Riding Institute for the Promotion of Fine Arts which opened on the 23 July 1827. The pictures were 'Heaving the lead, a sailor's frolic' [63] and 'View of the village and bridge of Grange' [64] but no surviving landscape or genre painting has so far been identified from his hand. Indeed only a single picture has so far been located; this is a canvas of the brig *Henry* in the Town Docks Museum, signed and dated *I. Willoughby, 1820* which is a very modest example of ship portrait painting (fig. 20). There are no identifiable portraits by John either but there are three by his father Robert Willoughby (fig. 21). [65]

Another John Willoughby carried on the family trade and is recorded as a painter and gilder living at 23 North Street with a workshop at 68 Osborne Street. He shared the North Street address with John Ward who had been living there since 1832. Clearly he was Ward's assistant or junior partner and when Ward retired from the more mundane aspects of business to concentrate on teaching marine art and preparing his lithographs he recommends John Willoughby as his successor. Resident at 2 Osborne Street in 1848 he is variously described as house, ship and sign painter;; painter and decorator; and house painter and paper-hanger. He died aged 39 in September 1858. [66]

WILLIAM BARTON (d. 1814)

Not primarily a marine painter this obscure individual active at the beginning of the nineteenth century has left us a number of interesting topographical pieces with a greater or lesser degree of nautical content. Recently acquired by the Ferens Art Gallery is a splendid representation of the river frontage at Paull with a Baltic trader in the offing and a view of Hull in the distance, it is dated 1809 (fig. 22 and pl. 12) [67]

A ship portrait by Barton passed through the London salesrooms in 1988 depicting the armed merchantmen *Lusitania* and *Hugh Crawford*. Inscribed Hull and dated 1809 (?) Humber keels can be seen in the distance and the river bank forms the horizon. [68]

His brief obituary notice in the *Hull Advertiser*, 20 August 1814, describes him as a panorama painter and a pair of small canvases showing the entrance to the river Hull and the citadel may well be connected with designs for a panorama. The figures lounging against the blockhouse wall are curiously elongated in a fashion suggesting that the artist was experimenting with perspective (fig. 23) [69]

The classic panorama was a large painted canvas erected within a circular building or tent and mounted on frames so as to totally surround the viewer. This type of display or entertainment can be traced back to the Irish artist, painter and draughtsman Robert Barker. Detailed topographical and historical scenes could be given the illusion of three-dimensional space, aided by top lighting, and they remained popular until the advent of the magic lantern and moving pictures. Historic examples do however survive in the Hague and at Innsbruck where they can be seen in their original settings. [70]

Barton was apparently the manger of Barker's panorama of London when it appeared in Vienna in 1801. It was the first panorama to be exhibited in Germany and toured from Hamburg to Leipzig (where it was seen by Goethe) and Prague before reaching the Austrian capital. Shown in a newly built wooden rotunda in the Prater it was not a great success and failed to excite the local audience. William Barton (variously referred to as Wilhelm Barton, Bartou or Barthou) married a local girl called Therese and purchased the rotunda to begin an independent career. He initiated the creation of a panorama of Vienna for which he made the drawings from a vantage point in the Katherinenturm (a tower near the imperial Residenz), though the final canvas was painted by two Viennese landscape artists Laurenz Janscha and Carl Postl. The three thousand square feet panorama was opened in 1804 to great public acclaim and in 1806 it was replaced by a panorama of Prague, again drawn by Barton and painted by Carl Postl. He took the Vienna panorama on tour to Leipzig, Dresden and Berlin, again with great success. The following year it was shown in Hamburg, Copenhagen, Stockholm and St. Petersburg and in 1809-10 to Frankfurt am Main, Munich and probably through Switzerland to Milan. Clearly he must have left someone else in charge for the latter part of the tour since we know that he was painting in Hull in 1809 and 1810. In that year a panorama of Gibraltar (drawn by Barton) was shown at the Vienna rotunda, and after his death in 1814 his widow continued the business. The panorama of Vienna was seen in Austria again in 1817 and in London in 1824 as well as Paris and Budapest. When Therese Barton died in 1838 it was bequeathed to the city of Vienna but no trace of it can now be discovered. [71]

Barton was in touch with Thomas Meggitt whom he supplied with patterns for interior decoration in the German fashion from Vienna (see below). We may surmise that he had gained his original training as an artist in the Meggitt workshop.

A number of panoramas were seen in Hull during

22. *A baltic trader off Paull, Hull in the background (26³/₄ x 35¹/₄ in.); William Barton, 1810. (Ferens Art Gallery).*

the nineteenth century including a panorama of the British Grand Fleet at Spithead, threatened by fire from the blazing man-of-war HMS *Boyne*, painted by Robert Dodd (1748-1818), marine painter to His Majesty. [72] In 1800 a 'Panorama of the Battle of the Nile' was displayed in 'Mr. Bakers large room at Market Place' for an entrance fee of one shilling [73] and in 1836 moving panoramas of the 'City of Jerusalem', 'The Voyage of Sir John Ross' and the 'Perilous situation of the Whaleships' were erected in Queen Street. [74]

In 1829 the 'Grand Moving Peristrephic Panorama of the Siege of Hull in 1643' was displayed at Kirkwood's Olympic Circus. Executed 'by native artists of the town' (unfortunately not named) to the designs of J. Earle, presumably John Earle (1778-1863) the Hull architect, sculptor and builder. The eight separate views, the first of which showed Hull from the Humber as it was in 1829, were painted on 3000 square feet of canvas containing over two thousand figures and took more than two years to complete.[75]

It may also be noted that George Chambers (1803-40) when he first arrived in London was employed by Thomas Hornor (17810-1844), son of a Hull grocer and of the Quaker persuasion. He was engaged in helping to paint the huge canvas dome of the Colosseum, showing a view of London on 46,000 sq. ft. of canvas. [76] Chambers also worked for a time as a scene painter at the Pavilion Theatre, a trade followed by that notable Sunderland artist Clarkson Stanfield. Perhaps the last great panorama to be seen in Hull was that painted and exhibited by Henry Redmore in 1858 (see below).

23. View of the South End, Hull (8 x 11¹/₂ in.); William Barton, 1809. (Ferens Art Gallery).

THE MEGGITT WORKSHOP: THOMAS BINKS AND WILLIAM GRIFFIN

As far as can be established Thomas Fletcher began the local tradition of marine painting which was then taken up by Robert Willoughby. The two family workshops would inevitably be rivals in the house, ship and sign-painting business but it is possible that Willoughby attended lessons at Thomas Fletcher's drawing school. Possibly like John Willoughby he also received some artist's training from Ibbetson but neither speculation can be confirmed by actual evidence. Willoughby's considerable output however cannot have failed to have influenced the next generation of marine painters active in the city.

John Ward is said to have been apprenticed to Mr. Meggitt, according to the biographical note published in the *Eastern Morning News* for 1883. It is a very brief outline and most of the statements can be verified so there is no reason to doubt its overall accuracy. The two other significant marine painters of the first half of the nineteenth century Binks and Griffin also served their time with Meggitt and after completion of their apprenticeship continued to offer their work for sale from his shop in George Street, Lowgate.

Thomas Meggitt was the son of Thomas Meggitt, a master mariner who was living at 6 Adelphi Court, George Yard in 1863 described as a gentleman. An apprentice and journeyman to William Benison, painter, the young Thomas succeeded his master in the business of house ship and sign painter soon after he reached his majority in July 1800. [77] The ship painting aspect of the trade seems to have lapsed or become an insignificant part of his activities and Meggitt was essentially a decorator. In 1812 he advertised to the public that 'he stains and paints rooms in the German fashion now so prevalent in London; and is in possession of patterns printed in Vienna to various designs for ceilings and walls togeher with a room furnished in his house done under the inspection of Mr. Barton of Vienna'. (William Barton, see above).

He undertook gilding, bronzing, varnishing and polishing and also informs the reader that he produces 'transparencies painted to any design and transparent tracing paper sold'. [78] His son Thomas Smith Meggitt apepars in the trade directories for the first time in 1823 and from 1835 the firm is styled Meggitt and Son. A magnificent trade card in the Castle Museum, York, designed by the younger Meggitt and engraved by Goodwill and Lawson [79] displays the name and address, 10 George Yard, in a cartouche flanked by the tools of the painters trade and a view of vessels in the Hull roads with the familiar buildings of Nelson Street and the waterfront. On the reverse is a complete tabulation of the range of services on offer 'embracing all aspects of house decorating and furnishing and supply of paints and colour' (figs. 24-5) [80]

Until 1817 the firm was based at 8 George Yard but from 1822 the directories give the address as number ten in this busy thoroughfare between Lowgate and High Street. The son, T. S. Meggitt, died on 19 November 1842 at the early age of 37, predeceasing his father, and was buried in the churchyard of Holy Trinity Church. [81] The vault has since been uprooted and lost though the inscription is preserved in a notebook which forms part of the church archives now in the County Record Office, Beverley.

The following commemorative verse is given in John Symons *Hullinia* (1872).

'For social intercourse was kindly prized
His temper like his colours harmonized
In decorative art he greatly showed
Whilst modest merit held him for her own'

The father died on the 9 April 1851 at the age of 79 and the shop closed down. [82] None of the Meggitt family

MEGGITT & SON,
PAINTERS,
JAPANNERS. GILDERS.
DECORATERS &c.
George Yard,
HULL.

24. *Trade card of Meggitt and Son, designed by Meggitt Jnr. and printed by Goodwill and Lawson of Hull. (Castle Museum, York).*

seems to have been directly involved in marine painting and indeed the only item shown by T. S. Meggitt at the Hull and East Riding Institution in 1827 was a japanned jar and stand. [83] The workshop and the range of skills developed there as well as the ready supply of colours and varnishes which were part of the stock-in-trade did however provide the basis for a practical training in the craft of painting. Thomas Binks, William Griffin and John Ward, who were to dominate Hull ship portrait painting when Willoughby became too old to practise, all received their basic training with Meggitt. Like Ibbetson who complained bitterly of the drudgery of his apprenticeship they probably acquired the special attainments of the marine painter by dint of application to the sketch pad in their own time and possibly by attending lessons at Robert Willoughby's evening drawing school.

Thomas Binks (1799-1832), son of George Binks, a painter, remained in the Meggitt workshop until 1828 which means that assuming he completed his seven year apprenticeship at the usual age of 21 he stayed on for a further eight years. A prospectus issued on 24 February 1828 is entitled 'T. Binks, Artist and Painter in general (late assistant to Mr. T. Meggitt) no.45 Salthouse Lane, Hull.' Like his former master he was a decorator and 'having left Mr. Meggitt in October last, he has since spent some time in London, for the purpose of becoming acquainted with the first fashions in practice, and also with decorations for rooms (never before introduced in this part of the country) which he pledges himself to execute in superior style'. [84] A copy of the prospectus folded over and inscribed 'Colo'l. Grimston, Grimston Garth' indicates that Binks was undertaking a job for this representative of an old Yorkshire family or at least had approached him in the hope of a commission. [85]

A number of early works survive, painted whilst Binks was at George Yard these include, the ship *East Indian* in the National Maritime Museum, Greenwich, signed and dated 'T. Binks, Pinxt 1819' (fig. 26) and the P.S. *Kingston*, signed and dated 1824 which is in the Town Docks Museum (fig. 27). The latter is probably

the work exhibited in 1870 as the 'First Steamboat on the Humber;'[86] belonging to Weddle and Brownlow this was the first *locally built* steamship to enter regular service on the Humber starting in 1821. A canvas of the P.S. *Kingston*, P.S. *Prince Frederick* and P.S. *Calder* of Goole'[87] also in the collections of the Ferens Art Gallery is attributed to Binks but is almost certainly a joint work with Griffin (see below). These are all straightforward ship portraits with only incidental features to enhance the composition, a buoy, a rowing boat, a hint of land on the horizon, but Binks produced a particularly fine study of the whalers '*Jane, Viewforth* and *Middleton*' beset in the Arctic. Signed and dated 1836 it records events in the terrible season of 1835 when five vessels were lost and the eighteen survivors returned with the produce of only thirty-three whales (fig. 28 and pl. 14).

It was shown by Mr. H. Robinson at the marine exhibition held at the Artillery barracks in 1883 [88]. In 1827, his last year with Meggitt, he showed two marine subjects at the exhibition of the Hull and East Riding Institution, these were a 'Marine view on the Humber, from the jetty at South End' and 'Sea piece off Dover'.

A canvas of the ship *Halcyon* which hung for many years at Hesslewood Orphanage is signed and dated 1832 and includes a three quarter view of the pilot cutter number 6, the *Duke of Wellington* (fig. 29). This same vessel shown from the same viewpoint, but reversed left to right, is one of a number of drawings on the now separated pages of a pocket sketch book which are preserved in the Town Docks Museum. None are signed but on the strength of this relationship with a finished painting signed by Binks, they can reasonably be assigned to his hand or at least to his workshop. A picture featuring the P.S. *Victoria* (launched 1837) gives an interesting view of the Hull waterfront (fig. 30).

Thomas Binks died on 10 November 1852 at the age of 53 [89] but was succeeded by his son Thomas Henry (b.1833) who may be responsible for 'Vessels in the Hull roads'. Signed T. Binks the date is indistinct but probably should be read as 1859. The style is however much like that of Binks Snr., the vessels shown in a sharply delinated, graphic manner and a sea with small

HOUSE & ORNAMENTAL WORK

executed in every department of **Decoration** *and after all the Varieties of*

Woods & Marbles, highly Varnished & Polished.

Gilding & Bronzing for **Frames, Room Mouldings, Figures, &c.**

Dressing Tables, Chairs, Bed & Window Cornices, & every description of Furniture, Japanned or Re painted to any Pattern.

INDIA CABINETS & SCENT JARS

repaired, cleaned, Varnished, Japan'd, & Gilded complete, or prepared, Varnished & Gilded for Ladies to decorate.

WIRE   *Window Blinds Painted*   **Papier Maché Decorations**   *& ORNAMENTED IN EVERY STYLE,*

in Corners and Mouldings for Rooms, Window Cornices, Flowers & Centre Pateras for Cielings,

in Gilding Bronzing & Colors.

DINING ROOM, HALL, PASSAGE & SINUMBRA LAMPS,

Chandeliers, Brackets, Finger Plates, Handles, Gas Decorations &c. re bronzed and lacquered

Pictures cleaned & Varnished.   *Plain & Fancy Gold Mouldings.*   *Maps and Prints Varnished.*

Work on Glass in Gold & Bronze for Show Bottles, Shop Windows &c.

Door & Finger Plates   **Room Floors Chalked for Balls, &c.**   *elegantly Japanned*

PAINT, OIL & COLOR   AT THE LOWEST PRICES & FIRST QUALITY,

& a particularly strong &c.   INVISIBLE GREEN, *prepared for Park Rails, Gates &c.*

Goodwill & Lawson Hull

25. Reverse of Meggitt trade card with a comprehensive list of work undertaken and stock in trade. (Castle Museum, York).

waves painted in a static decorative fashion. An unsigned and undated canvas of 'Whalers in the Arctic' attributed to Thomas Binks is an imaginative rendition of vessels in the norther seas rather than a ship portrait. The whale ship has a stilted somewhat antique appearance suggesting it may have been copied from an eighteenth century painting or engraving and the busy composition includes a whale hunt in progress and a vessel beset, with the crew on the ice.

Thomas Binks (Snr.) had a cousin William, partner in the firm of Green and Binks, painters, 195 High Street. Green had dropped out by 1831 [90] and the new style of William Binks and Son was adopted and retained until they ceased trading in 1863. In 1846 Binks and Son are described as painters, oil refiners and colour dealers with a processing works in Chapel Street, Sculcoates. They are listed as house, ship painters and decorators in 1848 and in 1851 more comprehensively as house painters, oil and colour dealers and varnish makers of 196 High Street with a manufactory at Oxford Street, Sculcoates. [91] Messrs. Binks and Son were represented at the Great Polytechnic exhibition of 1845 by specimens of Arabesque painting and an

example of fir stained in imitation of oak.

William Binks Snr. died in 1842 [92] and the business contained under the management of his son of the same name. No individual canvases or panel paintings bearing the signature of either father or son have been recorded but Binks Jnr. was commissioned in 1851 by the Rev. Charles Constable of Wassand to repaint the heraldic decoration of the south chapel in Lockington parish church. [93] The 173 shields originally painted on the panelling in 1634 trace the pedigree of the Estoft family and after the restoration was complete the artist added his signature 'Wm. Binks, Hull, pinxt' which is still clearly visible to this day. He is also said to have painted the theatrical backdrops recently discovered at Burton Constable Hall, relics of amateur theatricals arranged by Lady Marianne Clifford Constable and produced c.1845. [94]

It is interesting to note that Eliza Binks, sister of William Binks (Jnr.) married the Hull sculptor William Day Keyworth (Jnr.) on the 15 July 1840.

George Binks (b.1774) son of Benjamin Binks a cutler is listed in the 1839 directory as a painter of Grotto Square, Mason Street and his son George Binks (Jnr.), also a painter, at Chapel Street. The latter apparently gave up his trade for in 1848 he was a corporation beadle and he is still recorded as such in the 1871 census. George Binks (Jnr.) was the brother of Thomas Binks (Snr.) and another brother Luke Binks (b.1818) was also a painter. [95]

*26. Ship **East Indian** in two views (26 x 35 in.); Thomas Binks, 1819. (National Maritime Museum, Greenwich).*

27. Paddle steamer **Kingston**, Yarmouth roads in the distance (11 x 19 in.); Thomas Binks, 1824. (Town Docks Museum).

28. The **Jane** of Hull (in the foreground) with the Scottish whaleships **Viewforth** and **Middleton** beset in the Arctic, 1835 (26 x 36 in.); Thomas Binks, 1836. (Town Docks Museum).

*29. Ship **Halcyon** of Hull (25 x 36¹/₂ in.); Thomas Binks, 1832. (Ferens Art Gallery).*

*30. Paddlesteamer **Victoria** of the Hull Steam Packet Co., proceeding past the Hull waterfront; Thomas Binks, 1839. (Private Collection).*

WILLIAM GRIFFIN AND REUBEN GRIFFIN

William Griffin is one of the least well recorded of the local fraternity of marine painters though a considerable body of work survives, much of it painted on panel. William was probably the son of Thomas Griffin,[96] house and ship painter resident at Salthouse Lane with a shop on the north side of Queens Dock and later at 12 North Wall, in the period 1803-17. William appears in the directories for the first time in 1822 at 50 Dock Street where he remained until 1838. Latterly he moved to 5 Lumley Place, Anne Street. The latest entry is for the year 1848 and throughout he is described simply as William Griffin, painter.

An unsigned picture, oil on panel, of the P.S. *Lion* with the P.S. *Calder* of Selby, now in the Ferens Art Gallery, is attributed to Griffin. [97] In the background are the buildings of the port of Goole in its first stages of development as the company town of the Aire and Calder Navigation which dates the piece c.1825. The P.S. *Calder* a river steamer belonging to the Aire and Calder Co. appears in the same view and as a virtual replica in the large canvas of the '*Kingston, Prince Frederick,* and *Calder*' attributed to Binks. The vessels in the latter painting have the dry and academic precision typical of Griffins representations of early steamers (fig. 31 and pl. 13). On the other hand the sea with its regular little waves with their highlighted crests and the brightly painted sky with masses of cloud are characteristic of the work of Thomas Binks. The canvas cannot have been painted before 1822 the year in which the *Prince Frederick* was launched but not later than 1827 the last year in which the two men were both still working for Thomas Meggitt. It is possible also that Griffin and Binks were responsible for the scheme of mural decoration that was uncovered in the main upstairs room of the Lowther Hotel, Goole, in 1980. Completed in 1826 all four walls are painted with scenes of sailing ships in dock and of river steamers such as the P.S.

Caledonia and P.S. *Eagle* which are identified by name. The remainder of the room is decorated with various maritime motifs and the coat of arms of the Aire and Calder Co. which used to hold its regular board meetings there.

The earliest firmly dateable ship portrait by Griffin is the whaleship *Mary Frances* shown in three views and evidently commissioned by her master William Couldrey to celebrate his success in the 1832 season when he returned home with the produce of no less than 29 whales. [98] (fig. 32 and pl. 15). A canvas signed and dated at Hull 1839 depicts the sailing ship *Wanderer* in a rather crowded scene with the P.S. *William Darley* and several other sailing ships and steam craft in the offing. [99] The *Wanderer*, launched in 1836, was built and wholly owned by Edward Gibson of Hull until transferred to Scarborough in 1845 (fig. 33).

A rather less cluttered composition is seen in the picture of the ship *Herculaneum*, shown in starboard profile view against a view of Hull's waterfront. [100] Built in Hull in 1841 for Taylors of Liverpool she sailed from there to Calcutta and the picture is signed and dated *W. Griffin pinxt. Hull 1841* with the further inscription *T. Meggitt and Son, Hull* (fig. 34).

It may be noted that in the Grand Polytechnic exhibition in 1845 a canvas entitled '*Transit* and *Monarch,* steamers' was entered by T. Meggitt. This is probably the same piece which Griffin himself had shown in 1835 at the Exhibition of Fine Arts entitled 'The *Transit* and *Monarch,* Hull steamers off Heligoland.' [101]

The vessels of the Hull Steam Packet Co. (Weddle and Brownlow, later Brownlow and Pearson) feature in the panel of the *Kingston, William Darley* and *Gazelle,* all of them paddle steamers active in the 1830's. The *Kingston* appears in the joint production with Binks and the *William Darley* also features in the canvas of the

*31.`Paddle steamers
**Kingston, Prince
Frederick** and **Calder** in
the Humber (20 x 40
in.); Thomas Binks and
William Griffin c.1824.
(Ferens Art Gallery).*

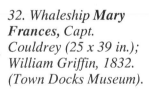

*32. Whaleship **Mary
Frances,** Capt.
Couldrey (25 x 39 in.);
William Griffin, 1832.
(Town Docks Museum).*

*33. Ship **Wanderer** with the P.S. **William Darley** in the offing; William Griffin, 1839. (Messrs. Christies).*

*34. Ship **Herculaneum,** off Hull; W. Griffin, 1841, on panel. (N. R. Omell).*

*35. Paddlesteamers **Rob Roy, Emperor** and **Queen of Scotland** belonging to Joseph Gee of Hull (19$^1/_2$ x 36 in.); William Griffin c.1848, on panel. (Town Docks Museum).*

53

Wanderer. The '*Jane* and *Harmony*' signed and dated 1837 was probably painted to mark the *Jane's* last voyage in the Arctic fishery in the previous season. [102] Both vessels had survived the most severe ice conditions and had returned home late in October 1836 without catching a single whale (pl. 16).

Several panel paintings unsigned and undated but undoubtedly from the hand of William Griffin depict paddle steamers of the fleet of Joseph Gee who at his death in 1858 was Hull's leading shipowner, owning a fleet of ships both in sail and steam. These panels are the simplest of ship portraits with no attempt at creating a setting and with each vessel shown only in one view, usually in profile. One of these depicts the *Queen of Scotland, Emperor* and *Rob Roy* all active in the Hamburg trade. [103] The *Emperor* built by Napiers of Glasgow in 1848 entered service the following year when at 914 tons she was, by a considerable margin, the largest vessel sailing out of the port of Hull (fig. 35 and pl. 17).

The panel painting of the P.S. *Helen McGregor* built for Joseph Gee by Laird of Birkenhead is signed with the monogram W.G. and the date 1843 applied to a boat hung on the port side davits. It is further inscribed *T. Meggitt, Painter Geo. Yard, Hull.* [104] Throughout his career Griffin clearly remained attached to Meggitt by whom his work was sold as dealer and agent no doubt with an appropriate commission for each item handled.

Griffin married Ann Cox at Holy Trinity Church on the 14 July 1822 and a daughter Phoebe was born in 1835 and a son Albert in 1840. He died aged eighty three years in 1883 whilst residing in Pease Street, and since the latest entry in the trade directories is for 1848 he must presumably have retired from business in middle age.

Reuben Griffin apparently another son, was also a painter who is listed in the trade directories for the first time in 1858 described as a house and ship painter, 9 West End, Queens Dock and from 1874-6 as a ship painter at $4^1/_2$ Dock Street. Many of the canvases signed

36. *The C.S.* **Alabama** *(right) and the U.S.S.* **Kearsage** *(left) engaging off Cherbourg, 1864; the S.Y* **Deerhound** *in the background (19$^1/_2$ x 29 in.); Reuben Griffin c.1864. (Town Docks Museum).*

by or strongly linked with Reuben are of an historical nature, recording battles at sea including a pair of panels of the engagement between the Confederate raider *Alabama* and the USS *Kersage* off Cherbourg in 1864. One depicts the two vessels in action and the other shows the *Alabama* sinking with the steam yacht *Deerhound* in the offing. Owned by John Lancaster a northern industrialist this craft picked up the surviving crewmen of the *Alabama* (fig. 36 and pl. 18). [105]

There was a more than passing interest by the representatives of local business and the Hull populace at large in the events of the American Civil War. Two cotton mills in the city employed over 2,000 operatives, at their peak of activity, though shortage of raw materials caused by the blockade of the Confederate ports by the Union navy resulted in the closure of the Kingston Cotton Mill in 1862. Sympathies were therefore largely with the southern states and the boarding officer of the *Alabama,* which in a period of twenty months had captured 71 enemy vessels, was a Hull man, George Townley Fullam, son of Capt. M. J. Fullam, master of the Hull Trinity House Navigation School, 1815-35. [106] A week after the dramatic events off Cherbourg the *Deerhound* visited Hull to take on coal before cruising off Norway and was the centre of great public interest. It is interesting to note that a public house at the corner of Chariot Street was renamed the *Alabama* and for many years showed a large sign over the door of the Confederate raider in action. Surprisingly the sign though entirely exposed was painted on canvas rather than panel as is revealed in a nineteenth century photograph (see fig. 1).

Reuben married Elizabeth the daughter of Andrew Brown a shoemaker on 8 September 1844 [107] and a son Charles was baptised in 1851. The earliest of his pictures, so far located depicts the steamer *Secret* and is signed 'R. Griffin 1850' while the date of his demise has not been ascertained.

JOHN WARD (1798-1849)

The outstanding Hull artist of the heyday of marine painting was undoubtedly John Ward (fig. 37). He was the son of Abraham Ward a master mariner and it is worth recording here the only biographical details of the artist published in the nineteenth century, though over thirty years after his death:

I am indebted to one of our local art connoisseurs for a few interesting facts respecting the marine painter John Ward, one of the few men of genius in the art world, who was born, lived, and flourished in Hull[108] - one of the worst nurseries, some may say, for a painter. Mr. Ward, I learn, was born here on December 28th, 1798. He was the son of Abraham Ward, master mariner, a native of Derbyshire, who in early life settled in Hull. He was apprenticed to Mr. Meggitt, house painter, and followed that occupation; but for many years previous to his death he devoted the whole of his time to marine painting. He lacked the opportunity of studying under a master, or in any of the great galleries, but, being an ardent admirer of the works of the late William Anderson, he copied several of them, soon, however, establishing for himself a distinctive style and character. For correctness in drawing and min-uteness of detail, especially in the rigging and sails of his ships, his works are unsurpassed by those of any other marine artist, but he excelled most in painting calms. His largest painting 'The Meeting of the Fleet at Spithead', is in the possession of Sir Edward Bates, Bart, of Liverpool, and many really fine specimens of his works are to be found in the collection of his townsmen, by whom they are highly esteemed. He also published some excellent lithographs illustrating 'The British Navy', and 'The Merchant Service', the drawings on the stones being his own work. He died at Hull, of Asiatic cholera, Sept. 28th, 1849. [109]

Abraham Ward appears as captain of the *Wolga* sailing for Elsinore and St. Petersburg in 1807 (*Hull Advertiser* 26 March). We also know that he married as his second wife Sarah Davies, a widow, at Holy Trinity Church on 16 August 1815 and died in 1836 aged 75 but otherwise we have no details of his life and career. A picture hanging in the Hull Trinity House, clearly painted by someone who understood ships and the rigging but was untrained as an artist, depicts the Hull whaler *Swan* in the Humber. [110] This is attributed to Abraham Ward and has led to the belief that the young Ward was inspired to paint by his father. Since the *Swan* was active in the fleet 1815-40 during which time the young man completed his apprenticeship and estab-lished his reputation this proposition is dubious. John's baptism has not been traced though the census return for 1841 indicates that he was born in the county. He was the second son of Abraham to bear this name the other died in infancy and is recorded in the burial register of St. Marys, Lowgate on 25 August 1795.

The assertion that he was apprenticed to Thomas Meggitt cannot be corroborated but is very likely to be correct since as we have noted both his contemporaries Griffin and Binks served their time in the George Yard workshop. Assuming he began his apprenticeship in 1812 at the age of 14 then he would have spent the next seven years not only learning the basic skills of house, ship and sign painter but would have developed his ability as a marine painter alongside these two men. The earliest work we can assign to Ward is a rendering in oils of 'The wreck of the troopship *Thomas*' on the Stony Binks off Spurnhead in 1821, [111] when he would have been 23 years old and out of his apprenticeship, though perhaps still working for Meggitt. It is not signed but the attribution to Ward is an old one and

*37. John Ward, self-portrait in regalia of Worshipful Master of the Humber Lodge;
destroyed by enemy bombing in 1941.*

there is no reason to reject it. The composition is good and there is evidence of painstaking effort to make an accurate record of an historic event (fig. 38).

A canvas of the whaler *Brunswick* signed IW 1823 was commissioned by William Blyth to commemorate the capture of no less than 36 whales during that season in the Arctic fishery and was donated to the museum in 1946 by the captains grand-daughter. [112] Wards mature works are generally signed in full and with a neat hand quite unlike this crude inscription. There is clearly an indebtedness to the established style of Robert Willoughby and it shows the same vessel in two views an arrangement the latter used most often. The ice floes are also rendered in a 'sugar candy' form reminiscent of Willoughby and the initials could equally apply to his son John whom we might expect to have picked up the same habit. The quality of brushwork is however greatly superior to that seen in a picture of the brig *Henry*, the only canvas positively identified as the work of John Willoughby. The execution of the whale-

boats and the figures are also far better than those seen in Robert Willoughby's canvases, the quality of the staffage and subordinate detail being a major characteristic of Ward's mature work. [113]

Acceptance of his first picture by the Royal Academy in 1831 is a landmark in Wards career. [114] This small panel is in private hands and shows a coastal scene with sailing vessels on calm water with fishermen hauling nets in the foreground (fig. 39). It is typical of the genre of marine painting introduced to Britain by the Van de Veldes in the seventeenth century and Ward joined this tradition by copying the work of William Anderson. The latter was a Scot who established himself in London where he exhibited at the Royal Academy for the first time in 1787 a piece entitled 'View on the Thames' and the next year ' A view near Gravesend'. It is interesting to note that Julius Caesar Ibbetson, the apprentice of John Fletcher and teacher of John Willoughby, was a close friend of Anderson and presented as his first academy picture in 1785, 'A view of Northfleet on the

38. Wreck of the ship **Thomas***, off the Stony Binks, 8 June 1821. (20 x 27 in.); John Ward, 1821. (Ferens Art Gallery).*

39. A frigate offshore with fisherfolk in the foreground; John Ward's Academy pice of 1831, signed and dated.
(Private Collection).

40. Shipping off Greenwich (19$^{1}/_{2}$ x 28 in.); a composition of William Anderson developed by John Ward, c.1825. (Ferens Art Gallery).

41. Stoneferry, with sloop-rigged keel (6$^{1}/_{2}$ x 9 in.); John Ward, exhibited in 1835. (Ferens Art Gallery).

Thames at Gravesend'. Ward acquired several of Anderson's paintings as we know from the inventory of the works sold from his studio [115] which lists two versions of 'Shipping off Northfleet' and a 'View of the Thames at Greenwich' ascribed to his mentor (fig. 40).

Significantly the three works which Ward lent for the 'Hull and East Riding Institution Exhibition in 1827 were all copies after Anderson entitled 'Northfleet', 'Limehouse Reach' and 'Sailing Match'. Ward presumably also managed to see the huge canvas by the Scottish artist depicting the 'Battle of the Nile' (1798) which was presented to the Hull Trinity House in 1813 but was subsequently destroyed. [116] Also belonging to Ward was a view of Mount Edgecumbe, probably the 'View off Portsmouth' by Ovenden lent to an exhibition at the Mechanics Instituttue in 1842. T. Ovenden is an obscure artist who exhibited a series of paintings of freshwater fish at the RA 1817-32 and is recorded at addresses in the Strand and Islington.

More interesting is a portrait of the whaler *North Briton* by Thomas Whitcombe (c. 1752-1824) which indicates that the London based artist must have visited Hull sometime between 1805 when the vessel was sailing in the Arctic fleet and 1824 when he died. His output was enormous and includes the series of paintings for the fifty plates of *The Naval Achievements of Great Britain* and his attention to nautical detail and understanding of ships and their rigging would certainly have appealed to Ward.

In 1835 Ward showed nine pictures at the Exhibition of Fine Arts including 'Stoneferry' and a 'View of Mr. Gleadows warehouse on Fire' taken from the Garrison jetty (fig. 41). Also included is a storm piece after Powell, Charles Martin Powell (1775-1824) is another interesting but little known artists whose identifiable pictures are scarce. He exhibited at the Royal Academy and British Institution 1807-21 but at his death left his wife and children in poverty. His paintings are characterised by the clarity of drawing of the vessels and well realised figures which are also attrib-

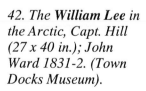

*42. The **William Lee** in the Arctic, Capt. Hill (27 x 40 in.); John Ward 1831-2. (Town Docks Museum).*

43. *Whaleship **Swan** (left) and the **Isabella** (25 x 35$^1/_2$ in.) probably Ward's Academy piece of 1840. (Hull Trinity House).*

44. Paddlesteamers Vivid and Waterwitch (18 x 27 in.); engraved by R. G. and A. W. Reeve, 1839, after an original painting by John Ward. Intended as a pendant to the print of the P.S. Wilberforce also belonging to the Humber Union Steam Packet Co. (Town Docks Museum).

46. The Maese, Amazon and Dandie Dinmont (10 x 14 in.); John Ward, 1848-9. (Town Docks Museum).

utes of the work of John Ward. Powell was a sailor apparently self-taught as an artist but influenced by the seventeenth century Dutch painter Ludolf Bakhuizen.

A copy of a painting of Calais pier by Powell in the first exhibition of the Hull and East Riding Institution for the Promotion of Fine Arts in 1827 was executed by a W. Coates, marine painter of Hull, who is otherwise unrecorded.

Another picture listed from Ward's studio [117] indicative of the variety of sources available to the artist is a seascape ascribed to Peeters, no doubt one of the family of this name active in the Low Countries in the seventeenth century, e.g. Bonaventura Peeters (1614-52) and Jan Peeters (1624-79).

The demand for ship portraits evidently grew as the century progressed and as we noted in the introduction both J. W. Carmichael (in 1829) and George Chambers Snr. (in 1827) received commissions to paint in Hull which no doubt acted as a spur to the local artists who were establishing themselves at the time. The 1830's were years of intense activity for Ward and he produced a quantity of panels depicting the entrance to the old harbour and variations on the theme of ships on the Humber. These were on a small scale with figures of mariners and fisherfolk introduced to great effect to lend colour, perspective and scale. They are generalised pictures of ships and the sea in the manner derived from William Anderson but with a bright atmosphere and with figures which are real individuals not just roughly sketched staffage to fill the composition. [118]

At the same time, and as his principal activity, Ward was producing ship portraits in which the principal vessel is usually depicted in two or three views. They would be painted to the order of a shipbuilder, owner or ship's master whose main interest was in the accurate delineation of his craft. Nevertheless Ward usually managed to create a satisfying composition with varying degrees of scenic interest. This is particularly true of the whaling pictures which contain a wealth of interesting subsidiary matter. The 'William Lee in the Arctic' painted in 1831 or 1832, for Captain Richard Hill, whose name appears inscribed on the whaleboat in the foreground, shows on the one canvas the entire sequence of the whaling operation from harpooning to flensing and the vessel itself in three views (fig. 42 and pl. 19) [119] This and his other whaling scenes of the period are all the more impressive for the magnificent treatment of the icebergs and floes and the accurate rendition of these features, not achieved by any of his local contemporaries, seems to indicate that he paid at least one visit to the northern seas in order to sketch the Arctic topography. The ships themselves were of course painted whilst in dock and perhaps sometimes with the aid of a builders draft (fig. 43).

Other compositions are considerably enhanced by the inclusion of Hull's waterfront in close up, as in the case of the 'Buoy yacht *Zephyr*' (c.1835), or from a longer distance giving a more panoramic view as in the 'P.S. *Forfarshire*' (1836 or 1838). [120]

The keen rivalry between the local steam packet companies particularly in the Hull-London cargo and passenger trade resulted in commissions to paint the paddle steamer *Victoria*, the *Wilberforce* and the *Vivid* and *Waterwitch* (fig. 44). Two of these were etched and engraved by R. G. Reeve and published as prints, the *Victoria* for the Hull Steam Packet Co. in 1838 and the equally splendid *Wilberforce*, in three views, was produced in the same year for their rivals the Humber Union Steam Packet Co. Hull's waterfront appears as a very attractive background to both of these acquatints. The magnificent original oil painting of the *Victoria* hangs in the Hull Trinity House and the river sparkling in the sun is captured in a manner worthy of the French impressionists (pl. 20). Two years earlier W. J. Huggins, marine painter to His Majesty, had provided a series of coastal views to decorate the interior of the *Vivid*, a further indication of the prestigious nature of these London steam packets. [121]

In 1839 Ward was commissioned to paint the 'Return of the William Lee' a vessel which then belonged to Thomas Thompson and George Liddell along with Joseph Gee who also managed her. Once a whaler and already recorded on canvas in this role, she is depicted coming into the Humber Dock basin after re-establish-

*45. Paddlesteamers **Queen of Scotland**, **Rob Roy** and **Helen McGregor** (24 x 36 in.); John Ward c.1843. (Peabody Museum, Salem, Massachusetts).*

48. Lithographic print, a ship of 375 tons, Merchant Shipping series (6 x 8 in.); John Ward c.1843. (Town Docks Museum).

*49. The brig **Wupper** off Spurn (24 x 36 in.); according to a label on the back of the canvas it was the last canvas worked on by Ward before his death in 1849. (Ferens Art Gallery).*

*47. Lithographic print of HMS **Britannia** (13 x 9 in.); John Ward c.1842. (Town Docks Museum).*

ing Hull's direct trade with Calcutta. It is an outstanding piece of work which shows the artist at the peak of his powers capturing a bright, calm January day with a wonderful play of light and shadow in a composition which is without doubt one of the finest marine paintings by any artist of the nineteenth century (pl. 26) [122]

The 'Chase and Dagger' was executed in 1839 for Joseph Gee when he was the port's leading ship owner. This scene of two handsome Baltic brigs is untypical of Ward in as much as the sea shows a heavy swell and the Chase leaning at a rakish angle to the wind handsomely displays the crest of Gee of Bishop Burton carved on the stern and also depicted on the flag at the foremast. [123] At this same period Griffin painted a great many of the Gee paddle-steamers, but Ward's lively rendition of the Queen of Scotland, Rob Roy and Helen McGregor', 1843, now in the Peabody Museum, Salem, Mass, outshines them all (fig. 45).

Fine canvases were also produced by Ward for smaller concerns; the 'Bark Edward and snow William' for William and Bartholomew Fowler Sutton, owners and masters; and the Ruby, Wanderer and Garnet painted for Priest and Son in 1844 or soon afterwards. [124] The latter were not a great company in numbers of vessels but were extremely enterprising and in 1845 sent the first vessel direct from Hull to China.

Ward married Esther Leonard, the daughter of John Leonard, butcher and cowkeeper, on 18 April 1825 at Holy Trinity Church and they had four daughters. [125] In 1839 an advertisement announced the dissolution of the partnership between John Ward and William Jefferson, this is not our man but another John Ward, painter, who on 7 December 1829 was married to Hannah Medd. There was yet another John Ward who actually described himself as an artist and was married on 10 December 1825 to Sophia Cooper. The marine painter it seems was in business at 103 High Street from 1826, if not before, and was living at 23 North Street in 1832.

Early in 1843 Ward announced his retirement from the profession of house and ship painter and recommends John Willoughby as his successor. [126] The latter is probably the son of John Willoughby portrait and landscape painter and appears in the trade directory for 1846 as a painter and gilder living at 23 North Street with a workshop at 68 Osborne Street indicating that he was living in Ward's house whilst working on his own account. Presumably he had been an assistant and perhaps latterly a junior partner before Ward finally relinquished all interest in the more mundane aspects of the painters trade.

From 1843 Ward was preoccupied with teaching as well as preparing a series of lithographs which were themselves part of a scheme to produce a manual for would-be marine painters. [127] To quote his own words: 'J. Ward, 23 North Street, Charlotte Street, having arranged his draughts and drawings is desirous of giving instruction in marine drawing as applicable to marine painting, and feels confident from his experience as a marine draughtsman to report such information as will ensure him the support of those anxious to obtain a knowledge thereof. Terms known on application, where specimens can be seen. Portrait of vessels accurately drawn and painted.' [128]

Handsome ship portraits continued to appear in the 1840's but the flow was much reduced compared with the productive years of the previous decade. A number of small panels were produced at this time which relate to the subjects which appear in his lithographs, for example 'HMS Britannia, at anchor with the fleet' and the 'Maese, Amazon and Dandie Dinmont' which was painted in either 1848 or 1849 (fig. 46) [129] Clearly he was using the drawings and studies for his lithographs as material to be reworked into the sort of seascapes which he had initially derived from the work of William Anderson and had then followed with scenes of anonymous ships on the Humber.

There is also a very simple profile portrait of the Rosetta, [130] one of W. and C. L. Ringrose's brigs in the Dutch trade, which is reproduced in a lithograph but reversed left to right. In the print it is used to exemplify the brig as a ship type and is not otherwise identified.

Though Ward's premature death prevented the completion of his projected guide for marine painters a large number of prints were produced some of which

*50. The brig **Wilberforce**
(18 x 24 in.); W. Ward,
1804. (Town Docks
Museum).*

*51. The White
Squadron at the Nore
preparing to sail (18 x
29 in.); Lieut. R. S.
Thomas, 1787-1853.
(N. R. Omell).*

were issued in batches with title pages and paper covers. A series of ten lithographs of naval vessels illustrating the various rates, up to a first rate man of war of a hundred and twenty guns represented by the *Britannia*, forms a distinct set. These are often found loose but at least one set exists cloth bound with leather spine and corners, the cover stamped in gold letters with the title 'Ward's British Navy'. Also bound with the latter is the artists lithograph of the bark *Raymond*.[131]

There are two introductory pages with text which begins 'A series of ten views of the several rates and classes of vessels in Her Majesty's Navy, lithographed in the tinted manner from drawings taken at the different naval establishments, by J. Ward and expressly executed as a work of information and instruction.' Unfortunately we do not know anything about our subjects visit to the south of England to make his preparatory sketches, neither precisely when or where he went, nor how long he stayed, but the results were outstanding. As well as the prints already discussed Ward lithographed a group of four views of HMS *Britannia* each 13 in. by 9 in., at anchor and underway, which are amongst the finest studies of a man-of-war ever produced (fig. 47 and pls. 27a, b). In 1842 he exhibited stern and bow views of this vessel at the Royal Academy along with pictures of a ninety gun ship and a first rate of 110 which were presumably examples of the original drawings for the large scale prints of the *Britannia* and the series of ten. The artists tour of 'naval establishments' must therefore have been in 1842 or before. His contribution to the local exhibition in 1842 of 'Objects illustrative of the Fine Arts' included, bow and stern view of HMS *Britannia*, a sketch in pencil of a thirty gun frigate and 'diagrams and drawings of vessels in watercolour'. To the same event William Ringrose lent 'View off Spurn', a Mr. J. James 'View on the Humber', George Robinson 'View of Hull', John Levitt 'Marine View' and there were two pieces 'View on the Thames' and 'River View and Shipping' from the Wharton Collection.

More naval subjects were shown at the Academy in 1843, featuring the *Britannia*, *Pique*, *Greyhound* and *Nautilus* and at the British Institution 1842-5 and 1847. Ward's most ambitious canvas also featured HMS *Britannia* along with units of the fleet at Spithead; signed and dated 1847 it measures 67 in. by 97 in., the largest he ever produced, and appeared at the Royal Academy in the same year. For many years it was in the possession of Sir Edward Bates (1816-96), the Liverpool shipowner and director of the Cunard Steamship Company who was also the son-in-law of Thomas Thompson, the Hull merchant and shipowner. After disappearing into an American collection the picture has once again returned to Hull.[132]

There are a large number of lithographs of merchant vessels and the intention clearly was to illustrate an example of each type of craft, both sail and steam, which traded out of the Humber and indeed out of any major port in the land. He no doubt excluded the classic local sailing barge, the Humber Keel, which appears so often as an ancillary subject in his ship-portraits because it was unique to this region and not generally encountered very far afield. The simplest prints show a profile view with the name of the type below and a short description of the set of the sail and state of the wind. In some cases the vessel is represented by more than one print when it is shown in different attitudes. The names of the artist and publisher are appended on the usual small sheets (6 in. by 8 in. picture area) but are absent from the larger sheets (measuring 15 in. by 10 $\frac{3}{4}$ in. overall) which include the same views but accompanied by a plan view, elevation and transverse section(s) recording the proportions of the mast(s) and yards. There are also a number of more elaborate compositions showing a particular carft in various views in the one lithograph again with title and one-line description, or in some instances several ship types together and similarly annotated. The small subjects in monochrome lacking a defined picture area can be found printed one above the other, two to a sheet. The larger prints are cream tinted and usually have the caption *Marine Studies* printed outside the picture area (fig. 48). A group of the latter bound in paper covers ($13\frac{3}{4}$ by 19 in.) was published by M. C. Peck, printer, Lowgate, entitled

*52. HMS **Britannia** and units of the fleet off Spithead (67 x 97 in.); Ward's Academy piece for 1847. (Private Collection).*

'Marine Studies of British Merchant Vessels Designed and Lithographed by John Ward, Hull'. The selection is preceded by a single introductory page followed by two sheets of monochrome studies, two to a page, and five cream-tinted prints depicting respectively a sloop, brig and ship in various views and finally an assemblage of merchant vessels of different types.

Ward published a print in 1845 to commemmorate the arrival of the bark *Wanderer*, the first ship ever to leave Hull with a full cargo destined for China. Owned by William Priest she sailed under the command of Johm Priest and returned with 55 tons of tea, unloaded at London. An oil painting of this vessel recently passed through Christies.

In 1847 another commemmorative print appeared this time recording the first Grand Regatta of the Royal Yorkshire Yacht Club. It was dedicated to Thomas Richardson the owner of the *Hilda* and winner of the challenge cup. A runner up was the *Whim*, owned by Joseph Gee, Vice Commodore of the RYYC from 1847 to 1851 and a member of the Royal Yacht Squadron. The following year Ward produced a print of the *Dandie Dinmont*, an iron schooner dedicated to George Cammell for whom she had been built at South Shields.[133] Ward's *Forfarshire* was also painted for Cammell who was agent for the Dundee and Hull Steam Packet Co. to whom the ill-fated vessel belonged.

Even at this time of his life when his reputation as a marine artist was fully established Ward was not too proud to acknowledge his humble origins as a house and ship painter. In 1848 Ward published a small booklet entitled 'The English Alphabet arranged for the use of House and Sign Painters, writers etc' which explained, with examples, how to construct various kinds of letters in due proportion. Neatly lithographed each page of letters is faced with a page of descriptive text, whilst on the reverse is one of his studies of ship types. Sadly whilst in this interesting and highly productive phase of his career Ward was stricken by cholera in the epidemic which devastated Hull in 1849.

According to an unattributed note he was in his usual health in the morning and at noon he went to meet some of his daughters returning by train from Bridlington. In the afternoon he took to his bed and died at eleven o'clock the same evening. [134]

He succumbed at his home at 2 North Street in the presence of William Settle his pupil and assistant and was buried the next day in the Castle Street cemetery mourned by his family and his fellow freemasons of the Humber Lodge. Ward who had joined the fraternity in 1827 was appointed worshipful master two years later and was secretary of the Humber Lodge 1838-9. He was also a senior provincial Grand Deacon of the Provincal Grand Lodge of the North and East Riding of Yorkshire from 1838 to 1840. [135]

He presented a self-portrait to the lodge where it hung until it was destroyed in 1941 when the Osborne Street premises were severely damaged in an air-raid. Thankfully a photograph has been preserved but two other self-portraits sold from his studio in 1854 cannot now be traced. Similarly no example is known to survive of a lithographic portrait he had prepared inscribed 'John Ward, Mr. (i.e. Marine) painter 1848'.[136]

Brother Dr. Bell gave the funeral oration which was recorded in the hisotry of the lodge as follows:

'No man enjoyed the confidence of the members more than Bro. John Ward. His character was marked by an honesty of purpose and strict integrity of principle. He was strongly attached to the Order, kind-hearted and noble-minded, and exhibited an energy and enthusiasm which never deserted him under any disarrangement, ever supporting principle against prejudice and maintaining the excellence of Freemasonry by the strictest observance of its precepts. The language of Holy Writ was with propriety applied to him, that a 'great man is fallen in Israel'. A link is broken, a light is extinguished. The Humber Lodge will regard his loss as the falling down of one of her strong pillars, and will lament as for the loss of one of her brightest ornaments. His body was laid in the grave in the burial ground of Holy Trinity Church followed by his family and forty of his brethren, and we sorrow to

*53. Paddlesteamer **Forfarshire** off Hull (24 x 36 in.); John Ward, c.1836-8. (Ferens Art Gallery).*

record the death of so estimable a brother. Peace to the ashes of Bro. John Ward; consolation to his children. The good he has done is present to our mind, and that good is free from the speck of alloy'. [137]

Mr. James Neal, of the Hull College of Art brought public attention to the decayed state of Ward's head-stone and in 1966 at the instigation of Commander A. J. E. Snowden it was removed to the safe keeping of the Hull Trinity House. Here in the western porch of the chapel it can still be seen with the inscription barely legible 'Sacred to the memory of John Ward, Marine Artist, who died September 28th 1849 aged 50 years.'

Membership of the Freemasons undoubtedly brought Ward into contact with potential clients. A small canvas painted in 1842 of the schooner *Dwina* and *Ellen Crawford* [138] passed down in the family of Robert Morley Sawyer a shareholder in the *Dwina* who was also a member of the Humber Lodge. [139] His other partners were George Cammell and Thomas Wilson soon to establish himself as Hull's greatest shipowner.

A second version of the *Wupper*, a brig in the Dutch trade belonging to W. and C. L. Ringrose, which had already been painted several years earlier, probably soon after its launch in 1842, was left in Ward's studio after his death. [140] This canvas now hangs in the Ferens Art Gallery and a label on the back tells us that it was completed by his assistant William Frederick Settle (fig. 49).

There appears not ot have been a will, not surprising considering Ward's sudden demise, and the contents of the studio were not dispersed until 3 February 1853 when Messrs. Oates Son and Capes 'received instructios from the Administratix'. [141] Since the artists wife had predeceased him this would have been Esther Leonard Ward his eldest daughter, one of three still living in Hull, Mary Ellen and Emma being the other two. Sarah Elizabeth, born in 1829 had married Leonard Clark and emigrated to South Africa in 1850, the year after her father's death. The sale catalogue lists paintings, drawings, lithographs, plates (for engraving) and lithographic printing stones. There were 99 lots of lithographs amounting to several hundred prints and each lot of up to 40 items sold for between 12s and 19s 6d. the highest price being paid for coloured examples. Only three of his drawings and watercolours were offered for sale and the rest of his studies and sketches were probably acquired by Settle. The oil paintings included the three marine studies by William Anderson which had been in Wards premises since at least 1827, and works by Peeters, Ovenden and Whitcombe as described above. As well as the self-portrait there were three other works outside Ward's usual range, a painting of a dog, a cattle piece, a crucifixion. The highest price for a single lot was the £21 paid for 'The Return of the *William Lee*' which since the original was presumably still in the hands of her owners must have been another version. There is a similar but simplified picture of this scene with some of the subsidary features removed in a private collection and another version which shows the *William Lee*, port side on to the viewer and deletes the brig *Consort* from the composition. Both the latter and the magnificent original canvas are now in the Ferens Art Gallery. There were no sons but Ward was survived by a brother, Thomas Abraham Ward (d.1865) and several paintings were passed down to the latters grandson, E. W. Stephenson, including the copy of Anderson's 'Blackwall, looking towards Greenwich'.

A certain William Ward was active as a marine painter at the turn of the eighteenth century and may possibly have been related to John Ward though such a connection has not been established in the local archives. William died aged 41 in 1802 [142] and is described in his obituary notice as 'Mr. Wm. Ward of this place, mariner, well known for his skill in delineating perspective representations of ships and vessels in an accurate and beautiful manner'. Only a handful of his pictures survive all in watercolour and each depicts a vessel in strict profile view with the sails drawn in a stylised manner giving a charming decorative effect very much in the eighteenth century manner. There is a watercolour of the Hull whaler *Truelove*, 1801, (pl. 28) and the merchant ship *Wilberforce* painted in 1804 (fig. 50) which are both in the collections of the Town Docks Museum. Three drawings of vessels from Salem, Mass. in the

Peabody Museum, are signed William Ward and are evidently by the same hand [143] which indicates that the artist painted them whilst still a mariner and who, latterly at least, was in the transatlantic trade.

The impact of William Anderson on John Ward's small scale seascapes is very obvious but the other influences which helped towards establishing his own individual style of ship-portrait painting is not at all clear. We know however that he copied a picture by Powell and owned another by Ovenden, two near contemporaries.

We know that J. W. Carmichael and George Chambers Snr. visited Hull in 1826 and 1827 during Ward's formative years. Chambers handsome canvas showing the *Spartan* off the Hull waterfront could well have formed a model for some of Wards paintings of the following decade. Ward had nothing to learn from Carmichael in terms of composition and knowledge of ship construction and the only link we can find between the two artists is a watercolour copy Carmichael made of the Hull artists lithograph of the *Dandie Dinmont* in 1848. [144] One imagines that the chief interest to Carmichael was that it was built at Shields, though owned in Hull.

In his latter years Ward was probably in contact with Robert Strickland Thomas (1787-1853) a retired naval officer and part-time painter. He had joined the service at the age of eighteen and was influenced by Capt. George Tobin an amateur painter who was a friend of Thomas Luny (1759-1837) an important figure in the history of marine painting in Britain. R. S. Thomas retired in 1815 with the rank of Lieutenant and settled in Portsmouth supplementing his pension by painting pictures of naval subjects. The two main features of a splendid canvas entitled 'the *White Squadron at the Nore*' are HMS *Britannia* and a cutter in full sail (fig. 51). The latter is borrowed directly from Ward's academy piece of 1847 ('HMS Britannia and units of the fleet at Spithead') whilst the stern three quarter view of *Britannia* is the same as that which appears in Wards lithograph, though reversed left to right (fig. 52 and pl. 27b). We can conjecture therefore whether Thomas copied from Wards finished work or maybe through friendship with the Hull artist had direct access to the original studies. Both men exhibited at the Royal Academy and in the year Ward showed his bow and stern views of HMS *Britannia* Thomas hung his canvas of the 'Battle of Navarino'. [145] It may be that the two men had originally met when Ward visited the south of England in 1842, or earlier, to make his sketches of the various types of warship used in the preparation of his print series and the Academy piece of 1847. A composition close to this was also made by Richard B. Spence (fl. 1850-75) though with a fortified harbour shown in the background and all executed in a racy somewhat slick manner.

Ward's plan for a comprehensive series of lithographs showing all the main types of merchant and naval vessels to comprise a manual for marine artists may have been influenced by the *Liber Nauticus and instructions in the art of marine drawing* published by Dominick and J. T. Serres in 1805. Much closer in time and in the style and content of the plates hoever is the *Vyftig Afbeeldingden van Schepen en Vaartuigen* by Philip Le Comte published in Amsterdam in 1831. This consists of 50 lithographic illustrations preceded by sixty pages of explanatory text and shows a whole range of types from cutters and schooners through to a man-of-war and paddle-steamer, with an occasional plate giving details of rigging. The presentation is very simple and as in most of Ward's prints all vessels are shown in profile (or three quarter view) with small craft in the offing to add to the pictorial content. Often there is a spectator on a section of coast in the foreground or a mariner hauling on a boat devices which are familiar from Wards prints as well as his seascape paintings on panel. The overall effect is very similar except that Le Comte's lithographs have a coarser stippling and lack the delineation of fine detail characteristic of Ward. Close contacts between Hull and Holland make it likely that Ward could have seen an example of Le Comtes work which was itself part of a long tradition in the Low Countries stretching back to the sixteenth century and the origins of marine painting.

Another compilation of prints of ship types is the well known series by E. W. Cooke (1811-80). Published in 1829 the sixty five plates entitled *Shipping and Craft* are etchings of merchant and naval craft and various Dutch vessels frequently shown in a harbour setting or beached. Each print is simply titled and is not provided with any explanatory text.

All but one of Wards lithographs was published by William Monkhouse, printer, of York. [146] The exception is the commemorative print of the *Dandie Dinmont* produced by the Hull printers Goddard and Lancaster in 1848. The usual signature is 'J. Ward del et lith' indicating that Ward not only originated the design but drew it directly on the stone or at least corrected the drawing after it had been transferred to the stone. A number of watercolours survive which are clearly studies for these prints but the subject is orientated in the same way as the final print which suggests a tracing was made on transfer paper which was then reversed onto the stone. The paper when applied to the prepared surface would then take up the impression reversed back to its original orientation.

The last time there was a major showing of Wards paintings in Hull during his lifetime was at the 1845 Grand Polytechnic exhibition. Two works were supplied by the artist himself, two by Joseph Gee (Marine view, the *Red Rover*; and Marine view, Cronstadt), two by a Mrs. Cussons, one by a Mr. W. C. Robinson and one each by J. Levitt, M. E. Peck, Capt. W. Sutton (ship *Edward* leaving port of Hull), Mrs. Carneley (The *Victoria* steamship) and T. F. Reimer (Brig off Spurn).

At the 1862 exhibition of the Hull School of Art, Bethel Jacobs, silversmith and local philanthropist; W. H. Moss, mayor of Hull in 1856 and solicitor of the Hull Dock Company; Martin Samuelson, shipowner; J. W. Leng and J. England all showed examples of his work. In 1864 also at the Hull School of Art exhibition in the Mechanics Institute, Mr. J. Simpson lent two pictures and M. W. Clarke a single canvas. Michael Wrangles Clarke of Winterton Hall who as an active member of the Humber Lodge of Freemasons in the period after Ward's death built up a choice collection of the former Worshipful Masters paintings. These included the *William Lee*, probably acquired from the estate of Joseph Gee, the schooner *Juno*, the *Bee* revenue cutter, ship *Raymond* which were all sold in 1887 when the contents of Clarke's house were dispersed. There were also a number of unspecified naval subjects which were probably lithographs and 'Shipping in a calm' by W. D. Penny.

Other local individuals owning Ward pictures were Mr. E. Smith who lent three pieces to the Working Mens Art, Industrial and General Exhibition in 1870, and J. L. Jacobs who lent a single item 'The Humber' to the exhibition by the Hull Literary and Philosophical Society in 1878. In 1883 'the ship *Wanderer*' the 'Old Trinity House yacht' and the '*Bee* Cutter' all belonged to J. E. Hall (1827-91) of Barton on Humber, owner of the Hall's Barton Ropery. These were displayed at the Marine Exhibition held in the Artillery barracks, along with 'Hull whaling fleet 1834', the 'Rescue of the crew of the *Brave* by HMS *Donegal* after Sir John Duckworth's action at St. Domingo', both belonging to Clement Good and 'Off Spurn Point' lent by W. Dyson of Princes Dock Street. In the same year at the Hull Yorkshire and Lincolnshire, Fine Arts exhibition, 'the Greenland fishery' and 'Revenue Cutter off Spurn Head' were lent by Charles Spilman Todd, the Town Clerk, the 'Ship *William Lee*' 'Ship entering the Humber', '*Juno*' and '*Bee* Revenue Cutter' by M. W. Clarke, 'Shipping' and 'Victoria Pier', 'Hull and Shipping' by R. Middlemiss, 'Hull and the brig *Helen*' by Thomas Sissons and 'HM frigate *Pique*' by B. B. Mason J.P. Other pictures with only generalised names such as 'Marine View' were lent by Dr. J. W. Lunn, J. D. Holmes J.P. (two works), Robert Fleming and Miss Thompson. At the Hull Fine Art Gallery in 1889 F. Lambert showed 'the Revenue Cutter *Bee*' acquired from the Wrangles sale two years earlier. At the dispersal of George Cammells estate in 1858 were three Ward canvases 'A smart breeze off Spurn', '*Ellen Crawford* and *Woodville* off Heligoland' and '*Forfarshire* off the Pier, Nelson Street' along with two coasting scenes by Henry Redmore, then a young man still building his reputation. Cammell had been a close neighbour of Wards living at 6 Charlotte Street from where these pictures were sold by Mr. Charles Johnson the auctioneer (fig. 53).

WILLIAM FREDERICK SETTLE (1821-1897)

Born 6 March 1821, [147] the eldest son of Thomas Harris Settle (1789-1866) and Harriet Leonard, he was the grandson of William Settle, variously described as a builder or architect and surveyor (fig. 54).

T. H. Settle was baptised at the Fish Street chapel on 19 December 1789 and was married in London at St. Andrews, Holborn, on the 3 January 1820, the same year in which he was made a freeman of York. He was elected underclerk of the workhouse in 1824 and eventually became principal clerk to the governors of the Guardians of the Poor.

Harriet, like Esther Leonard, the wife of John Ward, is described as a butcher's daughter which makes it probable that they were sisters, though Ward and Settle have usually been described as cousins rather than uncle and nephew. A very useful sketch of Settle's life survives in a manuscript memoir which, though unsigned, was probably written by one of his grandchildren. Much of the information can be verified and it is undoubtedly a reliable source which tells us more about him than we are every likely to known about the other local marine artists.

Settle was educated at Mr. W. Barrett and Sons, Academy, Drypool Street, Great Union Street. As a result of an accident his tongue was injured and the resulting speech impediment caused him to avoid mixing with his school mates. Instead Settle found pleasure in study and was always very fond of reading and as a child his first efforts at drawing were to represent the various vessels seen on the River Humber or in the docks. [148]

His father was opposed to young William taking up art as a profession and apprenticed him to John Cragg, bookseller, printer and binder. The desire to pursue an artistic career was eventually satisfied, however, when he was made a gift of his indentures [149] after five years and at the age of twenty Settle entered the studio of John Ward, [150] firmly established by then as Hull's foremost marine artist. Surprisingly this is the only mention of Ward that appears in the memoir and it gives no indication of any family relationship between the two men.

Settle's father was a nephew of Samuel Ringrose of Cottingham Grange, member of an old East Yorkshire family of landed gentry and kinsman of William and Christopher Leake Ringrose, notable Hull shipowners active in the Dutch trade. [151] Settle Snr. seems to have been largely disowned by his uncle, after making a marriage the latter disapproved of, but this family estrangement seems not to have affected William. It may be partly as a result of this family connection that Ward received a number of commissions from the Ringrose family between 1842, shortly after Settle became a pupil, and his death in 1849.

William married Sarah Andrews, who ran a toy shop and was the daughter of a painter and decorator, on the 12 March 1857 at Sculcoates parish church. Soon afterwards they moved to London where the young artist, now in his thirties and a sound training behind him, hoped to make his fortune. Prior to leaving Hull he had taught at the School of Art held in the Mechanics Institute, George Street, which was situated a short distance from where he and his parents were living at 2 North Street [152] which had been Ward's house and studio (fig. 55). Settle was paying rent to Esther Leonard Ward the owner of the property. Ward himself had originally rented the house from a certain Mary Clark but by 1846 the property was his own.

Settle was an honorary member and the official marine artist to the Royal Yorkshire Yacht Club [153] which no doubt helped him to maintain contact with his home county when living in London. In 1851 he published a print, lithographed by T. G. Dutton, the outstanding marine print maker of the day, showing the

54. W. F. Settle as a young man.

55. This is apparently Ward's house at 2 North Street. The photograph from a lost drawing by F. S. Smith is inscribed on the back 'Wm. Fred Settle, house in Charlotte Street', Hull. The Settle family occupied Ward's house after his death and the street was subsequently renamed Charlotte Street.

56. Lithographic print by Day of the RYYC Regatta 1851 after a drawing by Settle (11$^1/_2$ x 18 in.). (Town Docks Museum).

*57. The frigate **Immortalité** and other vessels; W. F. Settle (Windsor Castle, Royal Library, ©1991. Her Majesty the Queen).*

58. Grisaille on panel, man-of-war and galley off a fortified coastline (4¹/₂ x 6 in.); signed and dated, W. F. Settle 1858, one of a pair. (Private Collection).

59. Settle oil painting in the Ward/Anderson tradition (8¹/₂ x 13 in.); signed with monogram, 1859. (Private collection).

RYYC regatta, clearly inspired by Ward's commemorative piece for the first regatta in 1847 (fig. 56). Leaving 2 Lismore Gardens (otherwise 2 Ventor Villa[154]) in the Hampstead Road, which the young couple had occupied c.1858-9, they returned to Hull for about four years which would seem to indicate that Settle had not had as much success as he had anticipated. Moving back to the capital again in 1865 the growing family made their home at 3 Grafton Terrace [155] where they remained until April or October 1868. He exhibited 'A Sea Piece' at the British Institution and this seems to be the only time Settle ever showed his work in a major public exhibition.

After the 1860's he abandoned oil painting and the sale of the many small but charming watercolours or crayons he executed must have brought only a meagure living to Settle. It was fortunate that a dealer or agent sent two or three examples of his work to Queen Victoria, who bought an illustration to 'Carmilhan', a poem concerning a phantom ship written by Longfellow in 1871, and another depicting a group of warships entitled 'Three Queens of the Sea'. [156] He was then asked to supply a number of drawings of warships of the Royal Navy to be used as Christmas cards. There is no confirmation of these transactions in the royal archives but two of Settle's watercolours do hang to this day at Osborne House, Albert and Victoria's favourite summer residence, on the Isle of Wight. These are entitled the '21 gun frigate, *Imortalité* and 'the yacht *Amber* and *Witch* with other ships' (fig. 57).

Despite his contacts with royalty, and according to the memoir, Edward, Prince of Wales and the Duke of Connaught, his brother, were also purchasers of his work, Settle never achieved any great national reputation though his work continued to be acquired by a number of Yorkshire patrons (pl. 29). The latter included Lord Londesborough, Charles Sykes, Joseph Soames, M.P. for Hull, Martin Samuelson, [157] shipbuilder, and Anthony Bannister, shipowner and coal merchant. He retained the friendship of Edward Bannister [158] (brother of Anthony) an old school chum who also became a professional artist. Several drawings of the Hull Citadel belonged to Sir Albert K. Rollit, member of parliament, and solicitor, subjects which were reproduced as rather crude chromolithographs. A number of his commissions relate to his links with members of the RYYC. From 1847-51 Joseph Gee, the Hull shipowner, for whom Ward had worked on several occasions, [159] was vice-commodore and in 1856 he was commodore with Anthony Bannister as vice-commodore. Gee was also a member of the Royal Yacht Squadron so could also have helped Settle find business amongst its members at their regular regattas at Cowes in the Isle of Wight. During his brief return to Hull he made drawings of the Humber Keel regatta, a fine pair signed with his WFS monogram and dated 1864, show the initial line up and the finish of the race.[160] Settle's confidence in handling oils seems to have declined as a result of problems with his eyes which began at this time. An infection nearly caused a loss of eyesight and prevented his working for several months.

The earliest oil from Settle's hand so far discovered is dated 1855 and there is a splendid pair, each $8^{1}/_{2}$ x 13 in., which can be dated 1859 (fig. 59). [161] In style these hark back to the Dutch tradition and a pair of grisailles each on small panels depicting seventeenth century warships in the manner of Van de Velde, show him to have been an outstanding miniaturist (fig. 58). [162] Another fine pair of pictures undated, but surely belonging to the same period, illustrate shipping on the Firth of Forth. Executed on board, only 8 in. x $15^{3}/_{4}$ in., they are minutely painted but at the same time conveying a marvellous impression of breadth and space. (fig. 60) [163]

Sadly his painting executed on a window blind to celebrate the royal visit to Hull in 1854 no longer survives. [164] Painting on transparent blinds of fine Scottish cambric and lawn prepared with isinglass or parchment size is described by Nathaniel Whittock in his book 'The Decorators, Painters and Glasiers Guide' of 1827. The two artists may even have met since Whittock prepared a Birds Eye View of Hull at the time of Queen Victoria's visit which was published by

60. Shipping on the Forth (8 x 15³/₄ in.); W. F. Settle, painted on board. (Private Collection).

62. Miniature pen drawings from a sketchbook (6 x 12 in., each page); W. F. Settle. (National Maritime Museum).

James Leng in 1856. A drawing of the pontoon built in 1849 for the Great Central Railway at New Holland is reproduced in the Hull edition of Barclay's 'Universal Dictionary' printed for William Sprent of Neville Street, c.1851. The volume also includes a print of the Arctic Whale Fishery clearly derived from Ward's picture of 'The *Swan* and *Isabella*'. A lithograph of the mariners almshouses erected for the Hull Trinity House in 1834 was probably intended as a book illustration maybe for one of the guides published by Cragg, his old master.

The yachting fraternity, whether in Yorkshire or the south of England, seem to have been the backbone of Settle's clientele throughout much of his career. The watercolours of the 1870's and 1880's survive in great abundance and invariably depict sailing warships, auxiliary steam warships and yachts in a variety of combinations. Obviously he was able to make regular sales of these pieces to the yachtsmen and ship lovers who frequented the Isle of Wight, especially for the great annual regatta at Cowes and the Spithead naval reviews. The cachet of some of his designs having been accepted by the Queen would no doubt have helped his sales and he continued to produce pictures in the same vein for the rest of his working life. According to the memoir he is said to have actually met Her Majesty whilst sketching the royal yacht but the precise date and circumstances are not recounted. An *oil* painting (probably one of his last) on board dated 1867 (or 1869, the last digit is not clear) shows the royal yacht *Victoria and Albert II*, HMS *Immortalité* the frigate *Warior* and a vessel of the Royal Yacht Squadron in the foreground; the Isle of Wight is seen from Spithead with the outline of Osborne House visible (fig. 61) [165]

A watercolour, dated 1878 represents an ironclad of the *Audacious* class, an ironclad frigate *Lord Warden*, a dutch vessel and a three decker. It is marked on the reverse 'marine painter to the RYYC' [166] and was owned by Sir Charles Allom, a keen yachtsman whose vessel the *White Heather* won the King's Cup three times, and the Royal Albert Cup on no less than seven occasions. He was the grandson of Thomas Allom (1804-72), to whom the drawing may have originally belonged, an architect and one of the founders of the RIBA as well as being a considerable topographical artist.

Two watercolour drawings dated 1882 were presented to a Mr. John Hayes of Hull, on the occasion of his marriage, by the firm of Stone, Settle and Wilkinson. Edwin Thomas Settle (1823-78) was William's younger brother who became a partner in this brassfoundry and the pictures he selected for one of his employees show typical combination of frigates, yachts and other craft. Arthur Wilkinson was himself apparently an amateur artist and a piece dated 1896 is also preserved by Mr. Hayes' descendants.

E. T. Settle showed two of his brother's works, entitled 'Morning' and 'Evening' at the 1864 exhibition of the Hull School of Art. William himself lent 'An American Clipper' and a series of monochrome sketches, W. H. Moss 'Return from the Review' and 'Off Woolwich', A. Bannister 'Marine View' and F. E. Friston (himself an artist) 'HMS *Cornwallis*'. Settle had shown his work for the first time in 1845 at the Grand Polytechnic exhibition to which he lent a watercolour described as a 'Fancy sketch' and another drawing entitled 'A schooner'. In 1862 he displayed 'Morning on the Humber' and views of shipping were lent by J. W. Leng and S. Friston. Two sea views appeared at the Working Men's exhibition in 1870, from Dr. Pyburn, and the 'Port of Grimsby' from C. Bannister. Only a single piece, 'Men-of-War off Spithead' was shown at the Hull and District Art and Industrial exhibition in 1878 and a 'Stormy Day' at the Hull Temperance Club in 1881.

The greatest number of Settle's pictures to appear together in his lifetime were put on display at the Marine Exhibition in the Artillery barracks in 1883. W. J. Robinson of English Street lent 'Regatta 1851', H. Robinson, Cogan Street, 'The Yacht *Kingston* winning Lord Londesborough's Race in 1851'. E. T. Sharp, Victoria Street 'The Three Queens' and W. Dyson, Princes Dock Street, 'Keel Regatta on the Humber, the start and finish'. Two untitled works came from W. Deaman, Berkeley Street, and eight more, two watercolours and six oils, from W. Kirk, Caxton Villa,

*61. Royal yacht **Victoria** and **Albert II**, HMS **Immortalité** and HMS **Warrior** (8 x 11¹/₂ in.); W. F. Settle. (National Maritime Museum, Greenwich).*

Derringham Street. At the Hull, Yorkshire and Lincolnshire exhibition in the same year, E. Howlett offered two marine views by Settle at thirteen guineas each and C. H. Bannister showed 'A View of Hull' and 'the Old Blockhouse'.

In 1883, Settle gave a watercolour of a '51 gun frigate in heavy weather' to the Victoria and Albert Museum, where it is still to be seen. This is the only major institution known to have acquired an example of Settle's work during his lifetime. A very interesting sketch book, also dated 1883, was presented to the National Maritime Museum in 1962 from the collection of his son Ian (fig. 62) [167] A watercolour of HMS *Sultan*, *Salamis* and *Valiant* is in a private collection in Beverley and a drawing executed in crayon and watercolours of the Hull Citadel dated 1886 in the Hull Trinity House. There are two versions of this and several oils which have been ascribed to John Ward which relate to these compositions. The Citadel had been demolished in 1854 so the drawing dated 1886

must have been copied from a study made many years earlier either by Settle or Ward. [168]

Failing health and eyesight rendered Settle incapable of work for much of the last ten years of his life but the author has seen watercolours dated 1887 and 1889 in a private collection. One depicts the familiar assemblage of sailing warships and ironclads and the other shows historic vessels of the seventeenth century. He had a family to support and declining faculties obviously put a strain on his finances. Already in 1877 he had moved away from the fashionable Hampstead area and was living at 14 Victor Road, Holloway. Latterly he occupied 34 West Green, Tottenham and this is where he died 3 March 1897 and he is buried in the local cemetery in an unmarked grave.

Settle is an interesting artist though not a great one. His early oils are finely exectued on a small scale and have real sparkle but such pieces were always going to appeal to the sort of audience, inevitably limited, who delight in the skills of the miniaturist.

Though he is said to have abandoned oil painting because of problems with his eyes this cannot be the whole truth since painting the fine detail of ships and rigging in watercolours would surely also be a great strain on his sight. The obvious reaction to such difficulties would have been to paint bigger canvases employing broader brushwork. Indeed large romantic seascapes, vigorous canvases with storm-tossed seas are just what the customer wanted at the time as was realised by Henry Redmore, his Hull contemporary. Evidently Settle was unable or unwilling to tackle this type of oil painting and so employed his talent for painting on the small scale, with modest commercial success, in the execution of drawings and watercolours. These inevitably had a limited appeal but he seems to have assiduously cultivated the yachting enthusiasts and patriotic ship-lovers for whom he produced in prolific numbers his pictures of yachts and warships. They cannot have fetched a high price and this meagre living ended rather sadly in an unmarked burial plot in Tottenham. He was the first Hull marine artist to leave his native town to pursue a career in the capital which he attempted with some seven years of tuition by John Ward and considerable local support behind him. Despite this his bright career prospects sadly failed owing to an inability to adapt to current fashion. His talent was not big enough to thrive in the metropolis and he was increasingly afflicted by poor health until his death at the age of 76.

HENRY REDMORE (1820-87)

Henry Redmore [169] was born at Hull in 1820 the son of James and Mary Redmore (fig. 63). [170] The father is described in the baptismal register as a house carpenter but we know from the report of the death of his wife in 1847 that he served as an engineer in the mill of Samuel Mann, mustard manufacturers of Reform Street, Hull. [171] Henry began his own career as a marine engineer and his first voyage was aboard the P.S. *Transit* of Brownlow, Lumsden and Co. The date is not recorded but assuming he started his apprenticehip at the usual age of fourteen this would have been c.1834. Redmore came ashore to take a post as an engineer with Messrs. Wright Bros. at the Cato mill situated in Trippett near North Bridge, Hull. [172] Again the date is not recorded but we may surmise that he left the sea at the time of his marriage in 1844 or soon after.

At what stage Redmore took up pencil and brush is also unknown but he is listed for the first time in a local trade directory for 1848 as a painter living at 4 Anns Place, Cottingham Terrace, just a short distance from his parents house at 9 Cottingham Terrace. Redmore senior is described in the same directory as an engineer. Ten years pass before there is clear evidence of Henry's artistic activity when the local press announces the opening of the Great National Panorama illustrating 'The glorious achievements of the British Navy commanded by the immortal Nelson'. [173] This work painted on 50,000 sq.ft. of canvas was displayed in the Grand Saloon of the Mechanics Institute in George Street 'together with a series of views of the most interesting and picturesque portions of the English coast in the British Channel and German Ocean'. The byline describes him as 'H. Redmore the celebrated marine artist of the town', a considerable boast considering that Hull's outstanding marine artist John Ward had been dead only nine years. The show was advertised from the end of August 1858 until the 25th September when the

last report indicated that it would be open for just a short while longer. Appropriate songs and music 'by talented artistes' regaled the visitors who were offered admittance at 3d, 6d and one shilling, children half price, the doors opening at 7.30 p.m. for commencement at 8.00 p.m. [174]

Two small canvases, signed and dated 1856 and 1857 which may have been included in this display both show fishing vessels and other craft off Spurn Point. [175] The earliest work so far discovered is signed with his initials H.R. and the date 1855 (fig. 64) [176] but there are two obviously juvenile pieces which are probably amongst the artist's very earliest attempts at painting in oils. One of these shows a rural scene with horses and a hay cart and the other Saint Paul the hermit fed by the ravens. Both are signed H. Redmore and executed on panel, [177] though not dated.

The question arises as to how Redmore acquired his skill in painting, was he self-taught or was he at some stage under the tutelage of one of the noted marine artists active in Hull when he was a young man? In 1843 John Ward had withdrawn into semi-retirement to devote himself to the preparation of a series of lithographs which it was intended should be assembled into a manual of instruction for marine artists. [178] Though this project was never completed a substantial number of prints were published and during the last years of his life, cut short in 1849 by the cholera epidemic, he advertised his availability to give tuition in the art of marine painting. [179] It is more than likely that Redmore was one of the applicants but there is no documentary evidence that this is so. Certainly a number of Redmore's canvases clearly demonstrate the influence of Ward but this in itself is not an indicator since what serious marine artist developing his talents in Hull at that time could have failed to be affected by the example of this gifted artist? (fig. 65) There are several views of Hull from the Humber painted in mid-career

63. Henry Redmore c.1870.

64. Merchantmen and other shipping in a choppy sea (14 x 21 in.); H. Redmore, 1855. (Private Collection).

65. Hull from the Humber (12³/₄ x 21³/₄ in.); Henry Redmore, 1874, a piece from the middle period but with strong echoes of John Ward. (Ferens Art Gallery).

*66. The S.S. **Gertrude** in the Humber (13¹/₂ x 22³/₄ in.); H. Redmore, c.1861. (Private Collection).*

which are made up of elements which were part of Ward's regular repertoire (e.g. 'A calm, vessels taking on provisions', 1870) but it is Redmore's more generalised riverscapes which most frequently echo his predecessors work. These are views of miscellaneous vessels on calm seas with conventional groupings of fishermen and mariners on the beach, a recognisable type of painting deriving ultimately from the Van de Veldes and the Dutch school of the seventeenth century.

A good example is 'Shipping becalmed', 1864, sold at Christies in 1986. It is probably such a piece that he described as 'Calm on the Humber', and exhibited along with another canvas entitled 'Fishing Ground in the North Sea' which was hung at the Royal Academy in 1868. [180] The latter item has recently been offered for sale by a gallery in Lancaster and features the smack *Confidence* surrounded by elements of the Hull fishing fleet. It can reasonably be surmised that the picture was originally commissioned by John Sims the owner of the *Confidence* and notable for introducing the box or fleeting system to the port of Hull.

Redmore had the advantage of a career afloat, even though it was of rather short duration, to enhance his understanding of the sea and ships and his training as an engineer would have involved some acquaintance with technical drawing. The general character of his paintings is however a romantic one whether of groups of vessels on calm sunlit waters or in violent storm-tossed seas and by rocky shores. There is no doubting his ability to paint ships in accurate perspective and with correct nautical detail but he was usually aiming for a spirited overall effect rather than painting an authentic portrait of any particular craft. There are a few ship portraits but these are as a rule very conventional, a simple profile view accompanied by a token piece of floating wreckage in the foreground to give added interest to the picture. Unlike Ward he seemed not to have possessed that particular flair to paint a well integrated scene, in which a fine ship portrait can be both enhanced by and subsumed within a balanced composition comprising topographical elements, figures and secondary features.

In his portrait of the screw steamer *Gertrude* ('A steam coaster') the starboard profile of the vessel tends to blot out the waterfront though an overall balance is achieved by means of the sailing vessels pictured on the left and the tower of Holy Trinity church rising up in the background. [181] The *Gertrude* built at Grimsby in 1855 was transferred to the Hull register in 1861 and was wrecked on 10th November, 1865 entering the port of Riga in the Baltic. Her principal shareholder was Zacharia Charles Pearson, mayor of Hull 1859 and 1861, a major shipowner who was bankrupted in attempting to run the blockade of the Confederate ports during the American Civil War (fig. 66).

Redmore's obituary refers to a picture of the schooner *Coupland*, 'taken whilst off Scarborough (which) will be remembered by many of our townsmen as one of his most prominent works'. [182] This incident on the afternoon of the 2nd November, 1861, resulted in the drowning of the crew of the Scarborough lifeboat *Amelia* which was dashed against the promenade. She had been launched to bring assistance to the schooner which had run onto the jagged rocks close to the Spa wall in a fierce storm. [183] The bystanders included Oliver Sarony [184] the noted photographer and Charles Lord Beauclerk, fifth son of the eighth Duke of St. Albans, both of whom risked their lives in a vain attempt to bring the lifeboatmen to safety. Beauclerk was dragged ashore in a semi-conscious state and died soon after. There are many versions of the event by Scarborough artists including a pair of oils by Ernest Roe [185] and a dramatic watercolour by J. N. Carter. [186] An exquisite little canvas ($9\frac{1}{4}$ x $15\frac{1}{4}$ in.) recently came into the hands of a dealer at Harrogate and in March 1987 was acquired by a private collector. Despite the small scale the drama is superbly caught with the mountainous waves and lowering skies. The scene is made poignant by the presence of a throng of spectators who assembled to watch, helpless, as the tragedy unfolded. There is no signature visible but possible traces of initials are apparent on the lifeboat and there is really no doubt that this picture is the work of Henry Redmore. The question arises however whether this is a smaller version of a

*67. Wreck of the schooner **Coupland** in Scarborough bay ($9^1/_4$ x $15^1/_4$ in); Henry Redmore, 1861. (Private Collection).*

68. The Texel pilot boat; Henry Redmore, 1869. (Messrs. Christies).

much larger original. Redmore frequently painted on a grand scale and this sort of subject especially of such a celebrated event would seem to demand one of his more epic canvases. It is however of the highest quality and certainly does not strike one as a record picture made by the artist simply for his own reference (fig. 67 and pl. 30).

Assuming Redmores picture to have been painted soon after the tragedy in 1861 it may well have been a decisive factor in establishing his predilection for stormy seas, craggy coasts and shipwrecks.

The obituary notice refers to another work 'The Texel Pilot Boat' as amonst his finest productions. [187] This is probably the work signed and dated 1869 which came up for sale at Christies in 1971 described as 'Men o'war and other shipping in a calm sea at sunset'. A feature of the painting is a pilot boat which is marked on the sail *Texel No.10* (fig. 68). A pair of pictures exhibited in 1883, lent by the Hull Seamens and General Orphanage record another historic wreck, the loss of the *Canton*. [188] One is entitled 'The barque Canton in a storm', and the other 'The barque Canton abandoned'. The latter survives, though in a much damaged condition, and a contemporary gilt label indicates that it was a gift to the orphanage made by Mr. F. Hudson in 1877. [189] Built by Dikes and Gibson of Hull in 1834 the *Canton* was altered from ship to bark rig in 1838. Purchased in 1857 by F. W. Hudson of Hull and Edward Hudson Jnr. of Sheffield in partnership with William Shepherd she was lost just three years later in December 1860 on a voyage from St. John's, New Brunswick.

Another canvas given to the orphanage by Hudson in the same year again shows one of his vessels, the ship *Salem*, signed and dated 1863. [190] A simple view in full sail it is somewhat stiffly painted. The large and really dramatic storm pieces were yet to come but in 1868 Redmore exhibited at the Royal Academy for the first and only time; two pictures were hung 'Calm on the Humber' and 'Fishing ground in the North Sea'. As mentioned above, the Humber scene is most likely one of the traditional riverscapes which had been part of the repertoire of the marine artist in Europe since the

seventeenth century. Possibly however it was a view of Hull from the Humber roads of which there are several versions including a huge canvas which now hangs in the Town Docks Museum which was apparently painted in 1876 though the date is no longer visible (pl. 31) [191]

A smaller variant with a slightly different viewpoint is in the Ferens Art Gallery, signed and dated 1874. The same collection also includes a watercolour copy of this dated 1885 bearing the monogram W.F.S. of William Frederick Settle. He had been a pupil and assistant of John Ward from c.1839 until the latter's death ten years later and was an almost exact contemporary of Redmore, in fact just a year younger.

Apart form the panorama of 1858, the earliest record we have of an example of Redmore's work being shown in Hull is a canvas entitled 'Shipping' lent by Martin Samuelson a local ship builder for the first exhibition of the Hull School of Art in 1862. The artist himself lent two works to the second exhibition in 1864 entitled 'Dutch fishing boats' and 'Dutch Market boats'. The artists increasing popularity and evidence of a large and enthusiastic local clientele is demonstrated by the entries in the Official Catalogue of the Working Mens Art, Industrial and General Exhibition held in 1876. No less than thirteen pictures were lent by eight patrons including G. F. Earle and A. Bannister. [192]

The titles of most of these works is typically imprecise 'Marine View', 'Sea Piece' and the like but scenes of Scarborough and the Scheldt are mentioned by name. Lacking measurements and with the general vagueness of titling it is usually impossible to follow the movement of individual Redmore paintings over the years. As increasing number of Redmore pictures have passed through the sale rooms we can often see the same work, given a simple descriptive name, resold within a very few years differently labelled (fig. 69). The titles are largely given according to the whim of the cataloguer and his varying degree of knowledge of ships and coastal topography. An important piece measuring 30 by 60 inches depicting *H.M.S. South-ampton*, which became a boys training ship on the Humber, was purchased by a dealer in 1969 and is now

69. The hay barge (25 x 37 in.); Henry Redmore, 1871. (Oscar and Peter Johnson).

*70. HMS **Southampton**
(35 x 60 in.); H.
Redmore, after 1868.
(Private Collection).*

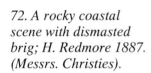

*72. A rocky coastal
scene with dismasted
brig; H. Redmore 1887.
(Messrs. Christies).*

71. Hull from the Humber (29 x 49 in.); R. Stubbs (and H. Redmore ?), prior to 1877. (University of Hull).

in private hands (fig. 70) [193]

There is not a great deal to say about the personal life of Redmore, he left no journal and the most informative sources are the obituaries published in the local press. These can be supplemented by the trade directories and gleanings from the parish registers. He married Martha Markham a local girl born at Newland daughter of Joseph Markham a labourer, on the 28 November, 1844, [194] and she gave him two sons and two daughters. Sarah Ann was the first born and is recorded in the census of 1851 as being five years old but died sometime before June 1872 when the death was announced of the second daughter Emily at the age of seventeen. [195] James Markham Redmore, the elder son, was baptised at St. Mary's Sculcoates, on 6th April, 1847, and is described in the 1861 census return as a stationer's errand boy whilst Edward King Redmore in the same year was only two years old. Edward's second name was borrowed from his uncle George King, a cooper, who had married Ann Redmore, Henry's eldest sister. [196] In 1851 George and Ann King, both then aged thirty seven, were occupying 8 Cottingham Terrace. James Redmore Snr. (actually spelled Redmoor) is noted in the census return as a widower aged sixty six and described as a visitor. The enumerator also records that he was born at Binbrook, Lincs. , and this has been confirmed by a search in the parish registers. He was baptised at St. Gabriels Church on 16 May, 1784, the son of George and Ann Redmore. [197] The Redmores seem to have been very close knit and Henry's elder brother Thomas, [198] who died aged fifty six on 24th July, 1872, lived with his wife Jane also at 8 Cottingham Terrace. [199] Jane was left a widow and died aged seventy two on 26th July, 1885.

In 1856 Henry Redmore was living at 62 Francis Street but had moved to 58 Norfolk Street by 1861. Two years later the trade directories list Henry Redmore marine painter, at 11 Norfolk Street apparently sharing the house with William Read 'A boot closer and shoe maker'. All of these houses were within a short distance of one another to the east of the Beverley Road. Cottingham Terrace ran along the Cottingham Drain, Francis Street a little further south running parallel to it. Norfolk Street is north and west of the latter passing between Liddell Street and the Beverley Road. As an indication of increasing income and status Redmore moved in 1863 to 6 Regent Street, off the Anlaby Road, [200] a thoroughfare now represented by Rawling Way which connects Hessle Road with Anlaby Road, entering the latter opposite Argyle Street. It was from this address he wrote the following letter on 16th April, 1870, presumably written to the secretary of the Royal Academy though the envelope with the addressees name is missing. [201]

Regent Street,
Hull.

April 16/70

Dr Sir,

I wish to thank you for your kind offer to receive my pictures for the Academy. I write to inform you I painted a pair but sold them and the Gentm. has sent them into the Academy.

I shall be very glad at any other time if you will allow me the same privilege.

Yours very truly,
H. Redmore.

Most successful and prolific artists, and Redmore was both, employed an assistant to help prepare canvases and sometimes actually participate in the painting of the finished composition. Vincent Galloway in his catalogue to the 1851 Festival of Britain exhibition at the Ferens Art Gallery tells us that Samuel John Spence (1842-79) whom he describes as a marine artist and landscape painter, worked with Redmore. Unfortunately he fails to give the source of his information and the obituary of this painter published in the *Hull Packet* (11 July, 1879) makes no such claim. [202]

It is equally likely that Redmore spent some time as an apprentice or assistant himself to one of the established local artists whilst he gained experience. Lot 87 of the collection of the 'Earle Gallery' of oil paintings sold at the George Hotel, 26th April, 1877 was 'A View of Hull from the Humber' attributed to Stubbs and Redmore. [203]

The former was presumably Ralph Stubbs Jnr. (1813-79) a close contemporary of Redmore who painted mainly views of the Yorkshire countryside in the northern part of the county and died at Levisham near Whitby. He also painted small scale picturesque views of ships on the coast and some accomplished sea pieces with lively assemblages of vessels reminiscent of Carmichael. A view of the Humber, signed R. Stubbs (29 x 49$\frac{1}{4}$ in.) with a type of composition and in a manner we usually associate with Redmore now hangs in the administration block of the Hull University and may well be the collaboration piece recorded in 1877 (fig. 71). It shows a close kinship with the views of Hull that Redmore executed in the 1870's which would perhaps indicate that Stubbs was in this case following Redmore but it is quite possible that the youthful Redmore had earlier turned to him for advice and instruction. Stubbs was brought up in an artistic environment, his father Ralph Stubbs Snr. (1774-1845) was a skilful landscape painter, and he would have gained his own accomplishment with the brush long before Redmore retired from a career at sea. Works by Stubbs were exhibited at Hull in 1862, 1864, 1870 and 1878 many of them owned by the same individuals we have identified as patrons of Redmore e.g. Martin Samuelson, A. Bannister and J. Patrick. A piece was also shown (posthumously) in the exhibition at the Hull Temperance Club in 1881 in a display of the work of local artists chosen by a committee which included Henry Redmore. A canvas by E. K. Redmore was shown on the same occasion. [204]

It is interesting that a record of payment in the archives of Burton Constable hall indicates that R. Stubbs received £6 for '*self and son* at 10s a day', in January 1844 though the nature of the work is not specified.

A number of canvases signed H. Moore, all undated, bear a strong resemblance in content, palette and atmosphere to the work of Henry Redmore. They are probably the work of the H. Moore, recorded in the Hull directories for 1895 as a marine artist living at 15 Marlborough Terrace, Hull. He would therefore have been a follower of Redmore, possible a pupil continuing to work in the former's style after his death in 1887. Moore's work is however considerably inferior, the brushwork often coarse and he had considerable difficulty in the placing of his vessels in convincing perspective. [205]

Another artist whose work shows close similarities to that of Redmore is William Calcott Knell. He flourished c.1830-76 but little is known about him. An even more shadowy figure producing works of the Redmore style is George Stainton, fl.1860-90, whose overall compositions are well balanced and atmospheric but the individual vessels are not well realised and lack substance. John Callow a London based artist who certainly painted on occasion in the north of England also worked in a similar manner though he was principally a watercolourist.

If, as the titles of a number of pictures suggest, Redmore made regular visits to Scarborough, it is quite possible that he he made contact with the eminent marine artist J. W. Carmichael (1799-1868) who was resident there from 1864 until his death. Carmichael was a prolific and influential artist and as we have noted, the work of Ralph Stubbs Jnr. (who hailed from North Yorkshire and may well have known him personally) show in a number of instances evidence of familiarity with the Newcastle artist's work.

We know nothing about Redmore method of working, whether he was an observer from the shore or perhaps revelling in sailing small boats perilously sketching whilst swept with spray. Only two drawings are known and these are probably records of finished paintings rather than preparatory studies. The larger of the two showing Dutch trading vessels and miscellane-ous craft is signed and dated H. Redmore, 1863. On the back is inscribed 'Becalmed, early morning in the estuary'. The second drawing repeats the main group of boats but reduces the width of the composition by deleting a number of the subsidiary vessels and restrict-ing the view of the coast-line. This is inscribed on the reverse 'Dutch barges in a calm', again demonstrating the flexible nature of the titles given to Redmore's pictures!

In 1870 Henry Redmore moved from his residence (and studio) in Regent Street to live in his second wife's home at 163 Coltman Street amongst a once imposing collection of substantial villas and comfortable Victorian town houses running between Hessle Road and Anlaby Road.

Martha Redmore was aged thirty seven at the time of the 1861 census and must have died soon after for on 9th May, 1870, Redmore, himself aged forty eight, married Ann Hopwood, a widow of forty two and daughter of George Best, spirit merchant. [206] A few years later one of his neighbours William Ford [207] a barge owner living in one of the more impressive villas near the Anlaby Road end of the street was to take a keen interest in Redmore's paintings. Four works including 'Hull from the Humber' painted 1876 and a view of Scarborough harbour signed and dated 1886 were bequeathed by him to the museum in 1926 along with a number of genre and landscape studies by various nineteenth century artists.

A number of letters survive which were written by Redmore from his new home but unfortunately the envelopes are missing and there is no indication of the identity of the recipient. One of the most interesting reads as follow. [208]

163 Coltman Street,
Hull.

May 2 / 81

My dear Sir,

I have great pleasure in informing you I am getting on with your pictures in fact one is finished and the other is long way on. One is a Trawler trying to beat off a Lee Shore. Ship in distance driving in, an incident in the gale on the 28 October, 1880 when many vessels were driven ashore on the Yorkshire Coast the other is beach and rocks with wreck driven in they are both of them as fine as anything I have ever painted they are also the cheapest pictures I have painted I have at least £30 from dealers for pictures like these I mean the pair but that is of no consequence if you like the pictures which I feel sure you will I shall be quite satisfied and pleased.

I am thinking of having a run over to London and bring them with me when finished but I will write to you again.

I am dear Sir
Yours truly
H. Redmore

Another dated a month later refers to his receiving a cheque for £20 in payment from a client:-

163 Coltman Street,
Hull.

June 2 / 81

My dear Sir,

I rec'd your cheque all right and obliged should have acknowledged it at once but I would wait till I rec'd case, I rec'd it this morning. There is some mistake with it he said he should want 2/6 for a case of pictures I took the lid of to let him see it was empty I wanted to pay him but he said he would not take it.

I am dear Sir
Yours very truly
[£20.00] (stamped as a receipt)
H. Redmore

Then follows a note on the subject of a painting he had been commissioned to execute:

163 Coltman Street,
Hull.

June 11 / 81

My dear Sir,

I believe when I wrote you I forgot to allude to the picture you wish me to paint I will put one in hand I think I know what will please you. Say I nice Sunrise or Sunset with cliffs and beach calm water vessels on the beach I mean fishing craft with figures a nice busy picture.

I am Dr. Sir you(rs) truly
H. Redmore

The final letter of the group dated the following year refers to the completion of a picture but whether the same one as referred to in the previous communication is not clear:

163 Coltman Street,
Hull.

May 13 / 82

My dear Sir,

I have finished the picture and I think you will like it. There is a trip from Hull on Monday week for four or five days all being well we intend going by it. Please say if you will be at home.

Yours very truly
H. Redmore

Redmore was active right to the end of his life and there are at least four canvases signed and dated 1887 which still survive (fig. 72 and pl. 32) [209]

He produced some of his most accomplished marines at this later period executed in a confident free manner but he was also producing some interesting beach scenes. These are in effect genre studies in which fishermen with their small craft and seaside cottages are the subject rather than ships on the high seas or rugged cliffs and storm-tossed waters (pl. 33).

Earlier in his career figures had appeard to some effect in various beach scenes usually as general staffage. Some attempts at bringing them to the foreground and giving them individual character were not successful and the depictions of fisherfolk at this stage were often coarse and clumsy. However a delightful pair of canvases signed and dated 1885 painted with a bright palette and precise brushwork show fishermen and their cobles at Staithes near Whitby and the beach at Robin Hoods Bay.

He suffered a heart attack and died on the 8th December, 1887 aged sixty seven. The burial register gives the cause of death as 'angina pectoris' and the entry is witnessed by his eldest son James Markham Redmore of 6 Spyvee Street. The cortege left his home at 1.00 p.m. on Monday, 12th December and the service at the interment was conducted by the Rev. James Sibree in the presence of his family, friends and patrons. These included William Barry, photographer of Helio House, 7-8 Park Street, Dr. Daniels (probably Charles Henry Daniels, surgeon of 3 Charlotte Street), Henry

Hare, fancy warehouseman, Henry Cammell, Hare the family solicitor, Dr. Finlay MacNab of 55 Great Union Street, Mr. Wheatley of Pontefract and Mr. Manners. The latter is described in an obituary notice as the 'eminent silk merchant of London' who had purchased 'Homeward Bound' and 'A Calm' at the Academy for £300. [210] These must be the two pieces already referred to as 'A Calm on the Humber' and 'Fishing Ground in the North Sea' which were hung in 1868 and are the *only* two works known to have been shown at the Academy. It is quite possible that the series of letters written in 1881-2 were addressed to this wealthy patron.

An obituary in the *Hull News* whilst repeating most of the information given by the *Arrow* includes the additional fact that Redmore had received a number of commissions from the Antipodes but unfortunately does not give the names of any of the clients. [211] An oil entitled 'Devon coast, Ilfracombe', was shown at the Royal Manchester Institutue exhibition in 1885, priced at £30. [212] In 1887 'A Breezy day off Scarborough' appeared at the Royal Birmingham Society's annual exhibition. [213]

Redmore's remains still lie in the Hull General Cemetery under a simple headstone carved with palette and brushes and inscribed 'In loving memory of Henry Redmore (Marine Artist) who died 8th December, 1887 aged 67 years'. He left a personal estate valued at £981.16s.1d which included the bequest of a gold watch, chain and appendages to his son Edward King Redmore and the household furniture, plate linen, china, books, pictures and other effects to Ann his wife.[214] Henry Hare, fancy warehouseman and W. D. Smith of Grimston Street, carver and gilder, the executors, were empowered to sell the real estate and invest the proceeds to provide an income of 12s per week for E. K. Redmore until aged twenty-one then to divide the income equally with his brother James. The will which was prepared by Redmore in 1878 was proved at York on the 9th February, 1888 by Henry Hare the sole surviving executor. Ann Redmore died on 28th September 1898 and bequeathed a life interest in the property at 163 Coltman Street to John Best, probably her brother, who

died in 1916. [215] The house still stands though empty and derelict. It is quite modest in size essentially two rooms upstairs and two downstairs with an extension at the rear providing an extra room on both levels. These seem rather cramped quarters for an active and prolific artist but there is no indication that he at any time owned a studio apartment independent of his residence.

EDWARD KING REDMORE (1859/60-1941)

E. K. Redmore followed in Henry's footsteps as a marine artist and a number of early works were painted with considerable skill in a manner very close to that of his father (figs. 73-4). Subsequently the work degenerates as he became increasingly addicted to the bottle and he often dashed off a piece just for the price of a drink. It is ironic therefore that the only time his work was accepted for formal exhibition was in April 1881 in the rooms of the Hull Temperance Club. [216] This display of works by local artists, both amateur and professional was chosen by a committee chaired by the Rev. H. W. Kemp and including the mayor Alderman J. Leake, W. D. Keyworth Jnr. (sculptor) and Henry Redmore, his father; the honorary secretary was Charles Mason. Pictures were offered for sale by George Cammidge, the Withernsea topographical artist, T. Tindall Wildridge, historian and amateur painter, F. Somerscales and also Frank Pettingell, architect and designer of a 'Birds Eye' view of Hull published that year. Unpriced were three views of the Humber by Ward, 'A Calm Day' and 'A Stormy Day' by Settle and two canvases by Henry Redmore 'To the Rescue' and 'The Lifeboat'. Sculpture by Charles Mason and W. D. Keyworth was also on view and a painting by E. Chandler was exhibited by C. Holditch of Park Street whom we know possessed two canvases by Henry Redmore in 1883. E. K. Redmore showed only one picture, entitled 'Homeward Bound' which was offered for sale at £4.10s. including frame and glass (fig. 74) [217] As a rule he signed himself E. K. Redmore but a good example of his handiwork in the Ferens Art Gallery is signed in the bottom left corner with a monogram of the three letters, E.K.R., sharing a common vertical stroke.

There are some pictures which record the topography of the Humber bank. A view of Paull is close in spirit to his father's 'Hessle on the Humber' of 1869 but the vast majority of canvases that are known are thinly painted and shown an endless repetition of a few themes. A very common subject is a group of fishing boats in calm waters which frequently bear Yarmouth registration letters. There are in private hands a pair of pictures painted on millboard, signed and dated 1904, which show the *Crane* and *Mino* (fig. 75). These were two of the steam trawlers of the Gamecock fleet, victims of the Russian Outrage on 21-22 October that year. The *Crane* was sunk, the *Mino* badly damaged and part of her shell-torn companion-way is now exhibited in the Town Docks Museum. These pictures are very basic not to say primitive and are the latest dated words known if we exclude a childishly executed watercolour signed and dated 1937 [218] when he was seventy-seven years old. It depicts the sailing ship *Conway Castle* off Cape Horn in 1878.

E. K. Redmore died at the age of eighty-one on 23 December 1941 [219] at 4 Crystal Avenue, St. Georges Road, off Hessle Road the home of Hull's fishing community. Previously he had occupied 12 Cornwall Gardens, Wheeler Street, also off Hessle Road and in 1888 was at 41 Day Street, off Great Thornton Street, Anlaby Road. He was buried at the Western Cemetery, Spring Bank, in a plot already occupied by his son Harold who had died many years before at the early age of twenty-five. [220] Edward's baptismal record has not been found but he was born in either 1859 or 1860 the former date being suggested by the entry in the 1861 census return which records him as being at that time two years old.

A photograph of him as a young man aged about eighteen or so, stylishly dressed in a bowler hat, was taken by a Grimsby photographer and another taken in middle age at Ramsgate are both preserved in a family album. The implication, supported by the fact that so many of his later, and inferior works, depict fishing smacks with Yarmouth registration numbers, is that

73. E. K. Redmore c.1910.

74. *Homeward bound (20 x 30 in.); E. K. Redmore, c.1881. (Messrs. Sothebys).*

75. *The steam trawler* **Crane** *(H.246); E. K. Redmore, 1904, oil on board. (Private Collection).*

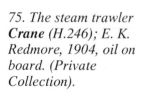

Redmore not infrequently left Hull to seek commissions at various ports along the east coast, particularly those with active fishing fleets. [221] A number of marine subjects painted on dinner plates have been seen by the writer which regarded as examples of folk art are very appealing but are otherwise another sad reflection of the artist's decline.

JAMES WHELDON (1832-95)

A James Wheldon appears in the trade directories living at 2 New Garden Street in 1863-4. He is either identifiable with the individual who married Isabella Heldt 23 December 1826 in Holy Trinity Church or more likely their son of the same name, baptised on 7th November 1832. It is curious that a James Wheldon, painter, is recorded marrying a *Sarah* Heldt on the 20th July 1822 at Sculcoates Parish Church.

In 1867 the firm of Wheldon and Warren, house and ship painters of Bourne Street are listed but the only Wheldon individually named in the same year is a Frederick Wheldon living at 3 March Street. Marine paintings are known signed F. Wheldon M.P. (fig. 76)[222] and the probability is that he was the brother of the younger James. A James Wheldon, painter, was at 21 Porter Street in 1876.

A number of canvases in the Town Docks Museum bear the signature of J. Wheldon (fig. 77) including pictures of the *Diana*, *Chase* and *Abram*, [223] three whalers active in the Hull fleet in the 1850's and 1860's, and also the P.S. *Seagull*, dated 1878. The *Diana* is depicted amidst an arctic scene of icebergs and floes with men in active pursuit of seals, walrus and whales. It is a busy composition and the naivety of its execution, especially the figures, adds to its charm. The initial of the signature is not entirely clear it could be Jas. or may be J.H. as appears on a painting of the S.S. *Edith* (1881); H presumably for Heldt his mother's maiden name.

A rather more polished version, the staffage reduced in prominence but with a large whale in the foreground, shows the *Diana* in three views. Another canvas demonstrating Hull's keen interest in the America Gulf Civil War and particularly the activities of the Confederate raider *Alabama* shows that vessel off Gibraltar. Dated 1863 the signature again could be read as Jas. or J.H. (fig. 78 and pl. 34). A pair of very competent and workmanlike ship portraits, signed and dated 1873, of the *John Wells* and *Richard Moxon* belonging to the Goole Steam Navigation Co. passed through the hands of a London dealer in 1978 (fig. 79)[224] The two vessels are shown in strict profile in a heavy swell with small silhouettes of ships on the horizon and a hint of land.

A fine picture of the S.S. *Baidar*, provides one of a group of four ship portraits of vessels belonging to William Nawton Smith. Signed and dated 1871 it accompanies the *Ella Constance*, *Dagmar* and *Edgar* all in matching ropework frames. The other three are all from the hand of Henry Redmore and Wheldon follows them closely in style and presentation (fig. 80).

Another canvas signed and dated 1878 shows the iron screw steamer *Essex* belonging to Bailey and Leetham of Hull.

A painting, in oils on board, of the S.S. *Edith* is boldly signed J. M. Wheldon '81 and this may be the work of a son or other relation, though no other artist of this name has been traced in the trade directories.

The most remarkable example of Wheldon's work shows an assemblage of shipping and depicts some of the best known warships of the nineteenth century. Starting on the left is the steam yacht *Deerhound*, which though not a naval craft itself was on hand at the engagement of the *Alabama* and *Kersage*. [225] Then there is a Humber sloop and a Dutch hoy followed by the U.S.S. *Kearsage*, HMS *Shannon* [226] (screw frigate built 1855), the Confederate raider *Alabama*, HMS *Duke of Wellington* (first rate of 131 guns), [227] HMS *St. George* (first rate of 120 guns, built 1840), [228] HMS *Audacious* (iron clad battleship, built 1869) and HMS *Royal Sovereign* (iron clad turret ship) (fig. 81 and pl. 35). [229]

A canvas signed and dated 1893 contrasting the old and the new, a wooden wall and a modern warship, was given to Hull Museum by the artist's great granddaughter in 1957.

76. The ship **Dowthorp,** a Bailey and Leetham steamer in the offing (24 x 76 in.); F. Wheldon, the **Dowthorp** was built in Hull, 1854, for Beadle and Co. (Town Docks Museum).

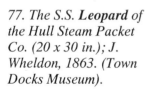

77. The S.S. **Leopard** of the Hull Steam Packet Co. (20 x 30 in.); J. Wheldon, 1863. (Town Docks Museum).

78. The C.S. **Alabama** *off Gibraltar (18 x 24 in.); J. Wheldon, 1863. (N. R. Omell).*

*79. The S.S. **Richard Moxon** (20 x 30 in.); J. Wheldon, 1873. (N. R. Omell).*

*80. The S.S. **Baidar** of Hull (33 x 50 in.); J. Wheldon, 1871. (Town Docks Museum).*

81. An assemblage of shipping (26 x 70 in.); J. Wheldon, 1872. (Town Docks Museum).

In private hands is a painting executed in the last year of his life signed J. Wheldon, in red, and dated 1895. It represents the S.S. *Austral* of the Ocean Steam Navigation Co. and was painted for the present owner's grandfather who worked on this vessel when in the employment of William Gray and Co. of Tilbury docks. [230] The death of James Wheldon, painter and decorator, in London on 6th of the month at the age of 65 is recorded in the *Hull News*, 14 December 1895. [231] If this is the same person baptised in 1832 the age is wrong by a margin of two years, but such discrepancies are common in newspaper obituaries of the period. Apart from misprints and incorrect recording people were often very careless about their birth dates and exact age. Often confusion may be caused by a delay between birth and baptism sometimes extending to several years. The *Hull News* 16 June 1900 records the death of Alfred Wheldon in his thirty-eighth year, youngest son of the late James Wheldon, marine artist.

WILLIAM DANIEL PENNY (1834-1924)

Born at Caistor, Lincs., in 1834 he is first listed in the Hull trade directories in 1869 but had presumably served an apprenticeship in the town before setting up on his own. He was living at 67 Francis Street c.1868-78, on Cottingham Road c.1882-9 and at 13 Newland Avenue c.1892-7 and is always designated as a marine artist, never a house or ship painter. At the turn of the century when he was advancing in years he removed to Aldbrough on the Holderness coast where he became publican of the 'Artists Rest', formerly the Bricklayers Arms; situated in Cross Street it is now a private residence (fig. 82). Penny continued to paint however, as a canvas dated 1910 clearly indicates, until he retired to a cottage in the High Street in about 1913 where he resided until his death in 1924. He lies in the 'overflow'

cemetery on the outskirts of Aldbrough.

An active painting career of about fifty years resulted in a prolific output and the Town Docks Museum possesses no less than fourteen canvases dated between 1866 and 1910 and the Ferens Art Gallery has another three. Most of these are simple ship portraits, the principal vessel shown in profile, though occasionally he produced a more interesting composition as in a study of Hull fishing smacks in the North Sea running before the wind. A number of canvases are designed to point the contrast between the old and the new, sail and steam, rather than characterising any specific craft. It is a great help that not only are his pictures signed clearly W. D. Penny but are invariably dated also which establishes a clear chronology for his work and enables

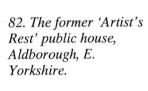

82. The former 'Artist's Rest' public house, Aldborough, E. Yorkshire.

*83. The S.S. **York** (20 x 35¹/₂ in.); W. D. Penny, c.1872. (Town Docks Museum).*

each ship portrait to be correctly identified. Penny's work is always competent and is an invaluable record of vessels sailing out of Hull in the second half of the nineteenth century. The great drawback however is that the canvases are often badly prepared and the thinly applied paint tends to flake. (figs. 83-84).

Passed down in the family of a Holderness farmer is a still life with fruit and a picture he painted of the great whale stranded at Aldbrough in 1900. Nothing is known about his antecedents but he married a Hull girl named Hester and in the 1871 census six children are listed, three girls and three boys. The eldest, fifteen year old James Walsham Penny is described as a fisherman, born in Leeds. [232] The remainder all born in Hull were still at school including W. D Penny Jnr. who was eleven at the time. Little of his work was publicly shown and indeed during his lifetime Penny's work appeared on view only at the 1883 Hull, Yorkshire and Lincolnshire exhibition. Two 'Shipping pieces' were lent by the artist and two others 'Shipping' and 'The

breeze off the coast' by a William Grindall.

Some years ago an oil of the Chilean warship *El Blanco Encalada* passed through the hands of the Parker Gallery, London. Built at Earles shipyard, Hull, in 1875, she was sunk in 1891, the first victim of the self-propelled torpedo.

A study of the *Diana* trapped in the ice, a moonlit scene, probably derived from the Widdas (q.v.) painting of 1867, was sold at Dee and Atkinson, auctioneers of Driffield (lot 842, 14 Feb. 1992) signed and dated 1889.

JAMES AND GEORGE WHELDALE (1839-55)

The earliest reference in the trade directories occurs in 1839 when J. and G. Wheldale, painters, are listed as having their business premises at 12 Bridge Street and a home address at 20 Canning Street. From 1842 they are described as house, ship and signpainters and are at West End, Old Dock in 1846 and North Side, Old Dock, in 1848. [233] After that date the two men seem to have ceased to work in partnership and James Wheldon is found living and working at 9 Garden Square, Princess Street, Mason Street, and George Wheldale was in business at Paragon Street but living at 30 Vincent Street. Between c.1846-7 George also traded as a licensed victualler at the *Grapes*, 38 Sykes Street. James disappears from the directories totally after 1851 and George is recorded for the last time in 1855 at 17 Grimston Street, as a painter, grainer and gilder. Mrs Mary Ann Wheldale, his widow, occupied the same house 1857-1861 and is also described as a painter. She is presumably identifiable with the Ann Atkinson who married George Wheldale at Holy Trinity Church, 3 July 1836. Several children were baptised there, Ann Elizabeth (6 May 1837), Robert (18 January 1839), Thomas (18 April 1840) and Emma (5 February 1842). Hannah Maria, daughter of James and Isabella Wheldale was baptised at Holy Trinity 7 September 1835.

The Town Docks Museum, possesses an oil painting of the sailing ship *Maida* of Hull, signed 'J. and G. Wheldale pinxt, 1839' (fig. 85) and in 1976 the 'Brigantine *George* off Spurn Point' signed and dated 1837 passed through a local saleroom. Their work is scarce and ship-portrait painting was probably not a major part of their output. Whether or not the Wheldales ever painted ship portraits individually is not known but J. Wheldale should not be confused with the better known J. Wheldon.

85. *The **Maida** of Hull (21$^1/_2$ x 28$^1/_4$ in.); J. and G. Wheldale, 1839. (Town Docks Museum).*

RICHARD DODD WIDDAS (1826-85)

He was the son of John Widdas, portrait and animal painter, born 1802 active in Hull and district and living at Barton-on-Humber in 1846. John died in 1858 and is buried in the Hull General cemetery. Richard is said to have been born in Leeds, 1 April 1826 and first appears in the Hull directories in 1858 described as a photographic artist trading as Widdas and Norris, 37 Bond Street. His home address was 10 Egginton Street and still at Bond Street in 1867 he is referred to also as a carver and gilder. In 1874 Widdas and Co., picture dealers, are at 14 Ocean Place and in 1882 his son George appears as a carver and gilder, picture and picture frame dealer at 6 Bond Street. The last entry for R. D. Widdas, describes him as an artist living at Walliker Street in 1885 and he died that year on the 28th or 31st December (fig. 86). [234]

Like his father he covered a wide range of subjects and the Hull museums and art gallery possess several coaching scenes, dated between 1869 and 1884 and three marines. One of the latter is a view of the Hull roads painted in 1879 and is a compilation picture showing the range of craft which frequented the Humber, from smacks and keels to the S.S. *Rollo* of the Wilson line. The composition lacks any real perspective and most of the vessels are depicted in profile. Another canvas of a marine subject is a very atmospheric piece showing the Hull whaler *Diana* trapped in the pack-ice. Seen by the light of the moon the crew on the ice having temporarily abandoned ship. Signed and dated 1867 it must have been painted soon after her return from a

87. The whaleship Diana beset in the ice, 1866 (24 x 36 in.); R. D. Widdas, 1867. (Town Docks Museum).

117

86. Richard Dodd Widdas. (1826-1885).

tragic sojourn in the Arctic which resulted in the death of her captain and almost a quarter of her crew. The bulky figure of her Surgeon, Charles Edward Smith and his Scotch terrier Gyp appear in the foreground. Through his journal, subsequently published, we have a detailed account of the harrowing events and the picture is probably based on sketches and descriptions given to the artist by Surgeon Smith (fig. 87 and pl. 37).

A third ship portrait in oils, signed and dated 1882, shows the Wilson Line vessel S.S. *Romeo* in starboard profile.

It is interesting that Widdas started his career advertising himself as a photographer but he seems to have abandoned the camera by c.1870 and the rest of his working life was taken up with painting and as a maker and seller of picture frames. During his lifetime only one example of his work seems to have been shown in public, this was a canvas of the 'Charge of the Light Brigade' in the Hull, Yorkshire and Lincolnshire exhibition of 1883.

Painted the same year as the *Diana* canvas is a lively rendition of the refusal of entry into Hull, of Charles I at the Beverley Gate, in 1642. In a private collection, it is signed and dated 'R. D. Widdas pinxit 1867'. The artist exhibited locally in 1870 several animal paintings and canvases with a religious theme.

A signed and dated picture entitled 'The Derby 1870' was sold as lot 81 at Sotherby's 28 October, 1964.

SAMUEL HENRY WILSON (fl. 1855-80)

Most of his surviving work consists of watercolour drawings painted on a large scale. Some of these were lithographed either by the artist himself or, in one instance at least, by William Monkhouse of York the lithographer and publisher responsible for producing most of John Ward's prints. No oil paintings by Wilson have come to the authors attention and no source indicates that the artist ever used this medium. The drawings were probably all conceived with the possibility of converting the subject into print form and many of the subjects depict vessels either constructed by C. and W. Earle at their Hull yard or owned by Thomas Wilson and Sons, in several instances built by the former and belonging to the latter. Wilsons rapidly expanded their operations in the late nineteenth century and when they acquired their biggest rivals, Bailey and Leetham, in 1903, they became the largest privately owned shipping company in the world with a fleet of ninety-nine ships. At the Art and Industrial exhibition of 1878 the company lent six watercolours the *Orlando*, *Hamburg*, *Quito*, *Hero*, *Calypso*, and *Orlando* all by S. H. Wilson and two oils by Samuel Walters, the Liverpool ship portrait painter, of the *Hindoo* and *Othello*. Since so many surviving examples of the artists work are associated with Hull's major shipping enterprise it is quite conceivable that S. H. Wilson was a kinsman of Thomas Wilson the founder of the firm, a local man born in 1792, son of a lighter owner.

In 1860, the artist was living in Liddell Street but appears to have been absent from the city for long periods. There are two drawings in the Chester Museum of the *Roodee* and *Robinson Crusoe*, both built in that town in 1863 and 1862 respectively for Beazley of Liverpool. Two views of the opening of the South West India Dock in 1880 are hanging in the premises of the Port of London Authority. These commissions could only have been executed on the spot in Chester (or Liverpool), and London. Wilson also made a drawing of the opening of the Albert Dock in Hull by the Prince and Princess of Wales.

The earliest firmly dateable works can both be assigned to the year 1855. A drawing dedicated to C. and W. Earle, her builders, represents the S.S. *Hawk* launched that year for John Raspin Ringrose of Hull (fig. 88). A lithograph by W. Monkhouse depicts another vessel the S.S. *North Sea* built by Earles to whom the print is dedicated, in 1855, for Thomas Wilson and Sons. Another lithograph, this time executed very skilfully by the artist himself, depicts the S.S. *Walamo* and is likewise dedicated to Earles the builders (fig. 89). She was launched for the Finnish Ladoga Steam Navigation Co. of St. Petersburg in 1859. The S.S. *Antelope* flying the house flag of Pearson and Colman depicted off the Victoria Pier, Hull, is another large scale watercolour (fig. 90 and pl. 39).

There are three nearly identical drawings known of the *Labuan*, built for Bailey and Leetham, which shows her engaged in the Arctic seal fishery. These can be firmly dated to 1861 since her one and only voyage to Greenland waters was made that year. The *Hull News*, 26 August 1871, refers to works by Wilson then being exhibited by Mr. Wells of Savile Street and states that he was commissioned to paint no less than seven paintings of the *Calcutta* for J. F. Norwood, the Hull shipowner, pictures of the *Cambridge*, *Dande*, *Winestead* and *Derby* for Bailey and Leetham, two portraits of the *Walamo* built in 1871 at Earles for Thomas Wilson and Sons, portraits of the *Marsdin* and *Dundee* for Humphreys and Pearson, shipbuilders of Hull and the whole of the fleet of Messrs. Horstedt and Garthorne. The report further remarks that some were of large dimensions up to five by three feet. Two ship portraits are recorded in the Peabody Museum, Salem, the S.S. *Olinda*, built at Earles in 1865 for Harrison of Liverpool and the *Artist* built at Hull in the same year. The *John Cropper* belonging to E. Powell and Co. of Liverpool recently passed through Christies auction house along with a view of shipping 'Off Spurn Head'.[235]

*88. The S.S. **Hawk** of J. R. Ringrose, Hull. (15 x 20 in.); S. H. Wilson, 1855. (Town Docks Museum).*

*89. Lithographic print of P.S. **Walamo** (13 x 21 in.); S. H. Wilson, 1859. (Town Docks Museum).*

*90. The S.S. **Antelope** of Pearson and Colman (25 x 33 in.); S. H. Wilson, c. (Town Docks Museum).*

THOMAS LUCOP (fl. 1867-1907) ; and CHARLES LUCOP (1828-1909)

The son of William Lucop, a master mariner, Thomas appears in the trade directories between 1867 and 1901. First as a painter resident at 38 Portland Street and in partnership in the firm of Hare and Lucop, at Earles Yard, 150 Osborne Street. Between 1872-5 he had a shop at 20 Day Street, but lived in Osborne Street. From c.1885 he was at 23 Trinity Street and then from 1889 he is described as an *artist* rather than a painter. At the turn of the century Lucop was resident at 51 Linnaeus Street and his last known address, in 1907, was 2 Park Street.

A fine painting of the paddle steamer *Hercules* passed through the hands of a London dealer in 1978 (fig. 91) and the S.S. *Earl of Dumfries* built in 1882 at Sunderland for Martin and Marquand of Cardiff is depicted on a canvas in the Welsh Industrial and Maritime Museum (fig. 92).

There are also a number of canvases which are not ship portraits but romantic scenes of shipping which are probably the inspiration for the style of painting shown by his brother Charles (fig. 93).

Charles Lucop (1828-1909) was a part-time painter and is rather better recorded than his brother. He went to sea as an apprentice but in the 1860's was engaged as manager of Reckitt's biscuit works at the Sutton Bank corner of Starch House Lane. [236] Later he was manager of the Peak, Frean factory at Barnstaple, Devon, and after returning from a year in South Africa briefly ran his own black lead business. He re-appears from several years of obscurity working as a ferryman taking passengers across the Queens Dock at halfpenny a trip. From about 1889 he was librarian of the Hull Mechanics Institute and later secretary too, an appointment which lasted about ten years until the Institute closed. He had attended the Hull School of Art, then held upstairs in the Public Rooms, Kingston Square and spent his leisure time painting pictures which he sold to supplement his income. A pair of oil paintings in the Town Docks Museum, each measuring $9\frac{1}{2}$ by 13 in. are entitled 'A Misty Morning' and 'Out of the Outer Manacles, Cornwall'; both are signed C. Lucop.

*91. The paddle steamer **Hercules** bound for Holland ($18\frac{1}{2}$ x $25\frac{1}{2}$ in.); T. Lucop. (N. R. Omell).*

*92. The S.S. **Earle of Dumfries** of Martin and Marquand, Cardiff (21 x 34 in.); T. Lucop: the vessel was built at Sunderland, 1882. (National Museum of Wales, Cardiff).*

93. Shipping in a calm sea (6 x 9 in.); T. Lucop, 1886. (N. R. Omell).

BENJAMIN TINDALL (fl. c. 1840-89)

His name appears in the Hull directories for the first time in 1840 when he is described as a tobacconist and painter, 13 Waterworks Street. Two years later he is listed as a house and ship painter, 11 Worship Street. By 1846 he had made the transition to marine painter having started his working life as a tradesman and we find him living at 17 Egginton Street before moving yet again, to 12 Lucas Square, Sykes Street, which he occupied c.1848-51. There is a listing in 1857 for a Mrs. Mary Tindall at this address, described as a lodging house, but another directory already has Benjamin at 79 Waverley Street in 1855. Latterly the address changes yet again to 4 Marlborough terrace (1885) and the latest entry in 1889 places him at number 67 in the same terrace.

There are no less than thirteen oil paintings attributable to the artist in the Ålands Maritime Museum at Mariehamm in Finland. These depict the variety of brigs, barkentines and barks owned in the Åland islands and which regularly traded from the Baltic into Hull (pl. 41). None of them have a conventional signature but some are characterised by a particular arrangement of three seagulls flying over the sea. In 1980 Gote Sundberg of the museum staff found a canvas, evidently from the hand of the same artist, but this time signed B. Tindall, thus enabling the artist responsible for this important collection to be identified at last. The painting preserved in a local farmhouse depicts the brig *Aura* built in Geta, Åland, in 1864.

Finland and the Åland islands were at that time part of the Russian domain and the craft depicted fly the white, blue and red imperial tricolour. [237] Only a canvas of the brig *Ida*, Capt. K. V. Letterman, 1876 bears a legible date but all in the group can be probably ascribed to the 1860's and 1870's and it was not until 1858 that the Åland boats started regular visits to Hull. The *Ida* is shown off Spurn Head with the Bull lightship in the offing and most of the other canvases include Spurn, with the high and low lights, and frequently a pilot cutter sailing nearby.

Another example, in the Peabody Museum, Salem, signed 'B. Tindall, Hull' and depicts the bark *Lois* which is probably the vessel of that name built in 1868 at Sunderland for owners in Aberystwyth. [238] An oil painting on panel of the P.S. *Transit* in the Town Docks Museum is attributed to this artist but no signature is visible (fig. 94). [239]

*94. The bark **Lois** (23¹/₂ x 35¹/₂ in.); B. Tindall, c.1868. (Peabody Museum, Salem, Massachusetts).*

W. R. NIXON (fl. 1870-86)

William Robert Nixon was another general painter but a number of his drawings and paintings have a maritime theme (fig. 95). The earliest work so far discovered is an oil painting of a topsail schooner signed and dated 1871 [240] and a small scale watercolour drawing of Joseph Gee's S.S. *Sultan*, probably extracted from a sketchbook, is dated 1877.[241] There is a fine portrait in oils of the fishing smack *Regina*, owned by C. H. Westoby, signed and dated 1883 (fig. 96) [242] A sketch book[243] contains drawings of fishing smacks, Wilson liners and various Goole steamships as well as views of Scarborough harbour, Whitby and Hornsea. It includes the drawing of a stranded dolphin, dated 10 September 1879, and there are also designs for interior decoration including heraldic notes and memoranda on the the use of colours. Dates applied to the various leaves range from 1876 to 1886 and there is a sequence of drawings of the various heats of the Humber Keel regattas of 1876 and 1877. His most polished production is a canvas painting of the Keel regatta of 1874 now hanging in the Town Docks Museum. [244] It shows the *Kiero* winning the Bailey and Leetham prize and was lent for exhibition at the Artillery barracks in 1883 by H. Robinson of Cogan Street (fig. 97 and pl. 42).

According to a tradition handed down in the family he is said to have been an intimate of Wilson's the shipowners, and to have been an observer of the notorious baccarat game at Tranby Croft in 1880*. Nixon restored the painting of the *Last Supper* by Jacques Parmentier (1658-1730) which was installed in the Holy Trinity Church in 1711.

95. W. R. Nixon.

*The Prince of Wales and entourage were staying at the home of Arthur Wilson during the St. Leger race week. On the evening of 8th September one of the party, Sir William Gordon Cumming, was accused of cheating and ultimately this led to a slander case being brought to trial with the Prince called into court as a witness.

96. The fishing smack
***Regina** (19¹/₂ x 27 in.);*
W. R. Nixon, 1883.
(Town Docks Museum).

97. The Hull Keel
*Regatta, **Kiero** winning*
the Bailey and Leetham
prize (20 x 36 in.); W.
R. Nixon, 1874. (Town
Docks Museum).

THOMAS JACQUES SOMERSCALES (1842-1927)

Born at Hull on 30 October 1842, he was educated at Christchurch School before attending the Normal College, Cheltenham, to train as a teacher. [245] The son of a master mariner, [246] he joined the Royal Navy to teach midshipmen afloat and in 1863 shipped aboard HMS *Cumberland* for voyages in the North Sea and the Atlantic. The following year Somerscales transferred to the wooden corvette HMS *Clio* which proceeded to the Pacific. Just before Christmas 1864 she put into Valparaiso, his first visit to the town, before sailing for the Mexican coast, Honolulu and Tahiti. Transferred to HMS *Zealous* Somerscales caught malaria in Panama and on 9 December 1869 he was sent into Valparaiso for hospital care and while there decided to buy his discharge from the navy and take a post in the Artizan English School run by Peter Mackay.

Throughout his time at sea, Somerscales had both sketched and painted watercolours. Now on shore Somerscales developed his skills in oil paintings of the Chilean scenery. His landscapes began to attract attention and, in 1872, he won a silver medal at the National Exposition in Santiago.

On 29 January 1871 he married Jane Harper [247] and carried on teaching at the Mackay Academy formed after a breakaway from the directors of the old Artizan school. Somerscales painted his first full-blooded marine canvas in 1875 and, in 1875-80, painted a whole series of subjects relating to events of the Chile-Peru War. In 1884 he won another silver medal at the Santiago National Exposition (fig. 98).

In 1890 the death of his daughter Alice had seriously disturbed his other daughter Sophia, and with his sons reaching university age Somerscales decided to return to England after almost thirty years abroad.

Though he returned to his native country as a totally unknown artist, his family provided a lively artistic setting for him. John Somerscales, his brother, a con-tributor to the Royal Academy, had painted a notable mural frieze for the Harris Institute in Preston, [248] while his sister was a friend of John Ruskin. Another brother, Francis, who is known to have painted landscape watercolours was a naval architect and general manager of Earles Shipyard, Hull, and could wholeheart-edly share his love of ships and the sea. [249]

Somerscales submitted his first piece to the Royal Academy in 1893 when he was aged a little over fifty years. The following year he started teaching in Manchester then moved to Acton in West London assisted by his brother Anthony [250] and sister Annie. While living in the metropolis he became a firm friend of W. H. Wyllie and J. J. Olsson [251] but in 1816 the school was closed and he returned to Hull, continuing his painting and regularly showing his work at the Royal Academy. His offering for 1899 'Off Valparaiso' was purchased under the terms of the Chantrey bequest and can be seen in the Tate Gallery. The next year, 1900, he undertook a tour of Europe, visiting Paris, southern France, Italy and Spain (fig. 99).

In 1903 'Homeward Bound', his R.A. canvas was brought by the Bank of Chile and Somerscales took the opportunity to return to South America and deliver it in person, but returned home the following year when his mother became ill. Further visits were made in 1908 and 1909 when he received a commission from the Chamber of Deputies for a huge canvas, some eighteen by fourteen feet, to hang in their debating chamber. After making a number of studies in Chile, he returned to England and it was executed in tempera on a frame set up in a shed in the grounds of Earles shipyard, courtesy of Francis, his brother.

Entitled the 'First national squadron' he took ship with it in 1912 and remained in South America until February 1915 when the events of the Great War persuaded him to return. Somerscales, however, con-

98. T. J. Somerscales, c.1885, when teaching in Valparaiso. (A. A. Hurst).

99. The 'Lame duck' (481/4 x 721/2 in.); T. J. Somerscales. (Ferens Art Gallery).

tinued to send canvases by sea to Chile during the war to satisfy a series of commissions. In 1918 he moved from the parental home in number three Leicester Street to Elmleigh, Princes Avenue. He sent his last canvas to the Royal Academy in 1924 when he was over eighty and died on the 27 June 1927 aged eighty five (fig. 100 and pls. 43-5). [252]

HARRY HUDSON RODMELL, R.I., R.S.M.A., S.G.A.

Harry Hudson Rodmell was born on the 28th May, 1896, the elder son of Henry Rodmell, butcher, of Holderness Road, Hull. [253] He attended Miss Walker's school on the Beverley Road and afterwards the Craven Street school where the idea of a career in art was encouraged by a Mr. Canham, one of the staff, as well as by Mr. Cooper the art master. He won a scholarship in 1911 to attend the Hull School of Art, Anlaby Road; this later became the Regional College of Art and is now part of the Hull College of Higher Education. (Latterly part of the Humberside Polytechnic, now the University of Humberside).

From the age of six he had demonstrated artistic gifts and delicate health caused him to spend more time with pencil and paper than might otherwise have been the case. Ships were a constant attraction and he would skip games lessons to take his sketch pad down to the docks. This early love of ships was the foundation of the deep knowledge of all kinds of craft which was to form the basis of his professional career. Whilst still in his teens he painted a picture of the S.S. *Eskimo*, the crack Wilson liner (launched in 1910), and this was bought by the directors of the company and used as the basis of a poster. [254]

Though eager to specialise and concentrate on maritime subjects he evidently took the advice of J. R. G. Exley, principal of the School of Art, to study art in all its aspects. This included developing a range of manual skills including woodcarving and two items he kept throughout his life are a carving of the arms of the City of Hull and the arms of Sir Neel Loryng. The latter, modelled after one of the stall plates in St. George's chapel, Windsor, was one of a series of heraldic plaques which earned him a commendation when exhibited in 1915. A lithographed heraldic panel also gained him a Board of Education certificate at the same national competition. In 1914 an illustrated broadside earned

him a national bronze medal at South Kensington. He also learned the technique of etching and a handful of small scale etchings dated 1919-20 are amongst the material left in his studio. One of these shows a merchant vessel at sea and another a group of warships at Scapa Flow. An undated series of topographical studies were etched for Forman of Nottingham probably to illustrate calendars or greetings cards. The principal urged him to try for a scholarship to study in Rome but he was determined to make his mark as a marine artist. In any case the war came in 1914, and he enlisted in the Royal Engineers so any ambitions as an artist had to be shelved for the duration. After demobilisation in 1919 he briefly joined a firm of lithographers in Hull but he was rescued from the routine of a printer's shop when he replied to an advertisement in the newspaper. Placed by a firm of London art, literary and publicity agents, Ronald Massey (later Carew, Wilson and Massey Ltd.) it sought an artist to prepare ship studies for poster and publicity material. This turned out to be the major breakthrough of his commercial career and throughout the 1920's and 1930's Rodmell received a regular series of commissions which established him in the front rank of poster artists of the period (fig. 101 and pl. 49).

In addition to his work for many of the great shipping companies such as Bergen Line, Blue Star, British India, Canadian Pacific, Finland Line, French Line (C.G.T.), General Steam Navigation Company, Holland-America, Norddeutscher-Lloyd, P and O, Swedish Lloyd and United America Line (fig. 102), he also provided some large scale studies, often double-page spreads, for the popular illustrated magazines of the period including the *Illustrated London News*, *Sphere*, and *Bystander*. He provided a series of pen drawings and gouaches for David Bone's *Lookout Man* which was first published in 1923 but though he was in constant demand to provide illustrations for a variety of periodicals this surprisingly was the only time his work was to appear between hard covers as sole illustrator, though several subjects appear in *Shipping Wonders of the World*. Commissioned in 1925 to paint the cargo liner *Oberon* for the Finland Line he sailed to Hull with her from the shipyard at St. Nazaire where she had been built. [255] The following year he collaborated with his friend Ern Shaw, cartoonist with the *Hull Evening News* in the design of a brochure promoting travel to Belgium published jointly by the London, North Eastern and London, Midland and Scottish railway companies (*Hull News*, 15.6.1926).

From March 1925 to November 1926 he contributed to the *Hull Daily Mail* a series entitled 'Humber Traders' (fig. 103) and from September 1927 to March 1930 'Guardships of the Humber'. A number of 'one-offs' were also published in the local press and on the 8th May 1926 a piece entitled 'Noble Brotherhood of the Sea' was interpolated in the sequence of 'Humber Traders'. The *Hull Times* for the 22nd December, 1928, reproduced an elaborate drawing of a medieval sailing ship accompanied by Christmas greetings from the artist. As a result of an introduction by Ern Shaw he produced a number of full colour pictures for Tower Press to use as subjects for their jigsaws. Some score of proofs for these remain in the artist's studio and subjects include the S.S. *United States* at New York, the liner *Queen Elizabeth*, as well as various recreated historic scenes featuring medieval sailing craft and harbour scenes both real and imaginary.

The range and quality of his work impressed Charles Pears (1873-1958), himself a Yorkshireman and born in Pontefract, and in 1939 Rodmell was invited to join him and other leading marine painters in a group that was to become known as the Society of Marine Artists, now the Royal Society of Marine Artists. The outbreak of war put a stop to its activities before it had really started to function but members of the SMA did make a showing at the United Artists exhibition held at Burlington House, Piccadilly, in January 1940, where one entire room was set aside for the work of marine artists. Another Hull artist who also contributed was his friend Allanson Hick, FRIBA, a practising architect who continued to produce marine studies until his death in 1975. Both men were elected members of the Society of Graphic Artists in 1937 and the previous year Rodmell was made a Fellow of the Royal Society of Arts.

In 1939 Rodmell had given to the Hull Museum of Fisheries and Shipping a splendid oil painting of the S.S. *Columbus* a liner launched at Danzig in 1922 and owned by Norddeutscher-Lloyd. Painted in 1924 he regarded it as his best work up till then and had reclaimed it from the shipping company by painting for them in return a picture of the *Bremen* the most recent addition to their fleet. [256] At the outbreak of war the *Columbus* was scuttled by her German crew to prevent her falling into allied hands and Sheppard, the curator, always alert to ways of publicising the museum transferred the picture to the central museum in Albion Street where it could be more readily seen by the general public. (*Hull Daily Mail* 28.12.1939). Fortunately it must have been returned to the maritime collections before the bombing raid in 1943 which destroyed the Albion Street museum, for it still survives intact as an outstanding example of Rodmell's pre-war style of marine painting (fig. 104 and pl. 48).

Throughout the Second World War he served with the Royal Observer Corps and also held evening art classes in Hornsea for members of the armed forces.

Already before the outbreak of hostilities he had been a part-time teacher at the Hull College of Art from 1931 to 1935. Wartime commissions were rather scarce and it is surprising that he was never called on, as were a number of his fellow marine artists, either as an offical war artist or to provide the subjects for the morale-boosting posters produced by various government agencies. His series of fourteen pen drawings of Humber guardships previously published in the *Hull Daily Mail* were however reprinted in the quarterly periodical *Bystander*, starting in October 1940 and ending in April 1942; two subjects each with a full historical description were put in each issue. His cover for the annual *Trade of Hull and the Humber Ports* was used from 1938 until

1946. A new drawing was used for the 1947 and 1948 issues. I can discover no other important works executed during the period of the 1939-45 war but 1943 was marked by a very important step in his personal life when he married Dorothy Thelma Fisher.

After the end of hostilities Rodmell returned to work for the shipping lines but the age of the great ocean liner had largely passed and the numbers of companies willing or able to indulge in elaborate posters and well designed publicity material had greatly diminished. Post-war orders did however come from the Euxine Shipping Co., Bergen Line, and the Hull-based firm Associated Humber Line. A regular task was producing an illustrated timetable for the tug company of William Watkins Limited of London. The museum has a series running from 1926 to 1951 followed by another series up to and including 1968 for Ship Towage, a company managing the combined fleets of William Watkins, the Elliot Steam Tug Co. and Gamecock tugs.

The thirty years after the war were probably the fullest and busiest of his life and he received a variety of marine commissions including a number of orders for oil paintings. These were often required before the vessel had been completed and he would work directly from the plans sent by the builders. An example of this approach is a picture of the trawler *Cape Trafalgar* launched in 1958 which he executed for Cook, Welton and Gemmell at the Beverley shipyard. (fig. 105). This canvas hung in the office foyer until the yard closed in 1977 and was for a number of years on loan to the Town Docks Museum. In Spring 1949 Harry Rodmell accepted an invitation to paint a picture of the *Port Brisbane* newly commissioned for the Port Line. He participated in the inaugural exhibition of the Society of Marine Artists at the Guildhall, London, opened on the 14th November 1946 by A. V. Alexander, formerly first Lord of the Admiralty, and at the time Minister of Defence. Earlier that year the Navy Art Exhibition had shown over seventy paintings by SMA members.

Despite the volume of commercial work coming in he managed to find time to paint subjects of his own choice and in a manner increasingly removed from the finely detailed studies usually demanded by his clients 'where every port-hole must be shown'. A favourite means of pictorial expression was line and wash either drawing the subject first and then adding the wash or applying the watercolour first and then drawing over it. A combination of both techniques might be used together, along with more than one sort of line on the same sketch, perhaps drawing with a carbon pencil and adding detail in pen and ink.

The arrival of acrylic paint on the artistic scene was welcomed by Rodmell and in his latter years when the hands were not as supple as they had once been the new medium was much more fluid and easier to work than oils. He also used acrylic paints in a diluted form which provided an ideal medium for an artist working with Rodmell's rapidity to produce pictures resembling watercolour drawings. These are often freely executed in a loose and confident manner which is never a substitute for lack of technique but an illustration of the freedom which years of disciplined work can allow the mature artist who knows his subject matter intimately.

Three of his drawings were on view at the annual exhibition of the Royal Institute of Painters in Watercolour in 1957 and that year he was elected a member, an honour which gave him a great deal of satisfaction. Rodmell's association with the RSMA remained close, he was on the council and frequently on selection and hanging committees for London exhibitions. He designed the emblem of the society which is used as a logo on their notepaper and publicity as well as being cast in silver as a pendant for the presidential chain of office. In 1979 he was elected as one of the very few honorary members, he also having been a founder member. His diploma work for the RSMA is entitled 'Royal Occasion'. This painting in oils shows a view of the royal yacht Britannia and her escort HMS *Malcolm* tied up at the dockside when the Queen visited Hull to officially open the Queen Elizabeth Dock on the 4th August, 1969 (fig. 106). It was first shown at the Ferens Art Gallery in 1970 and later that year at the annual exhibition of the RSMA in London.

101. Harry Rodmell in his studio, 1920's. (Mrs. D. T. Rodmell).

102. Lithographic poster for Nederland Royal Mail Line. (Town Docks Museum).

For Brook Motors Ltd. of Huddersfield he painted a series of twelve historic aircraft which were reproduced in their 1965 calendar. Although aircraft had appeared as incidentals in some of the naval scenes produced in 1914-18 for the illustrated magazines this was the first and only time he painted them as a main subject though he had familiarised himself with the forms and silhouettes as a member of the Observer Corps in the last war. A number of full colour covers were prepared for the Austin magazine, 1961-3, depicting harbour scenes and views of historic towns such as York and Lincoln and a set of drawings was published in the Unilever house magazine *Port Sunlight* in Spring 1968.

Voyages with his wife along the coast of Norway in 1967 and 1968 filled a sketchbook which provided the basis for a number of marine studies in Rodmell's most accomplished manner; including 'North Norway' (1970) and 'Vesterälen at Brønnøysund' (ca.1979). The latter exhibits a considerable looseness and free-

dom which in 'Hammerfest, northernmost town in the world', a townscape rendered in dilute acrylic, moves towards abstraction. Rodmell also enjoyed holidaying in the Yorkshire Dales with his wife, and a number of topographical paintings, again particularly watercolours, were exhibited in the 1959's and 1960's. He also provided a number of the drawings of country scenes which were used by the *Dalesman*, to which his friend Frank Armstrong was also a regular contributor. Like Rodmell he also was captivated by ships and the sea and exhibited marine studies with the RSMA and in the local artists' exhibitions in Hull and various Yorkshire galleries. Rodmell designed a new cover for the Port of Hull magazine in 1956 and in the same year gave a fine painting entitled 'Windjammer' to be sold on behalf of the Lord Mayor's fund in aid of the refugees of the Hungarian uprising. At this period teaching was an important part of his activities and though now reaching normal retiring age he was generous with his time and energies, holding day schools and lecturing and demonstrating to local societies. He gave talks to the Bridlington and District Art Society and the Haltemprice Art Group and adjudicated at their exhibitions. The latter still awards the Hudson Rodmell cup for the member judged to have made the greatest progress in the year, and was for many years presided over by Frank Armstrong. He was an active member, along with Allanson Hick and Frank Armstrong of the Hull Art Club, later the Hull Art Circle, a group encouraged and fostered by Vincent Galloway, director of the Ferens Art Gallery, who himself was a highly competent portrait painter.

In 1945 he was invited to teach adult art classes at the East Riding Evening Institute (now the Hornsea Institute of Further Education) and continued to give three classes a week until for health reasons he had to resign in 1972. He was the inspiration for a large group of enthusiastic amateur painters in the Hornsea area who joined together to form the Hornsea Art Society of which he was president from its inception. In 1961 he organised a painting school at Longcroft, Beverley, and was tutor for weekend painting schools, at Sheffield, Doncaster, Lincoln, Nottingham, Newark, Melton Mowbray, Shrewsbury, Ludlow, Hereford, Wolverhampton, Darlington and York, some of which he visited three times or more. The location of these courses turned his attention increasingly to landscape and architectural subjects which he more and more often exhibited though never laying aside his marine painting. Again he never failed to join in local community enterprises and regularly exhibited at the shows held by the Friends of Beverley Minster, a proportion of the proceeds from each of the pictures sold going to the restoration fund. The artist provided cover illustrations for the magazine of the sailors orphanage, Newland, in 1930 (replaced in 1936 and 1956) and his design for the front cover of *Magpie* the magazine of his old school at Craven Street was used from ca.1920 and by Malet Lambert School its successor until 1969. The current guide to the parish church of St. Nicholas, Hornsea, also has a cover designed by Rodmell, the dedication to the patron saint of sailors enabling him to introduce a ship into the design.

A series of pen drawings formed the basis for the 'Evolution of British Deep Sea Trawlers 1881-1955' in an advertising campaign for the Association of Fish Meal Manufacturers which he produced for Morison Press Advertising Service Ltd. of Hull, and which ran through 1955-1956. In 1948 he prepared a series of silhouettes of trawlers built by Cook, Welton and Gemmell, the Beverley shipbuilders, between 1883 and 1948. These were reproduced as a chart in the company's publicity brochure which was brought up to date in a later edition with a silhouette of a 1952 trawler. Perhaps his last major commercial order was for a series of drawings with washes to illustrate a colour supplement entitled 'Britain's Third Port' which appeared in RCH, the house magazine of Reckitt and Colman. [257] These were again reproduced and sold in aid of the RNLI and the Missions to Seamen.

Rodmell's work appeared at the Salon de Marine in Paris and his watercolour 'Lincoln Cathedral from Brayford Wharf' was selected for a travelling exhibition which went to the USA in 1965. The next year he was awarded a silver trophy at the Bridlington Art Gallery, Sewerby, for a drawing of an oil rig in Bridlington Bay. This was painted in dilute acrylic in the manner of watercolour. He received the silver trophy yet again in 1969 for an oil painting entitled 'Beam sea roll'. 1971 was the year in which the Hornsea Art Society held their first exhibition which was hung in the Vernon Gallery, Hornsea. Rodmell contributed that year but the onset of ill health prevented his presence in 1972.

Rodmell had made various contributions to the displays within the Hull Museums and in 1948 drew a cover illustration for the revised catalogue of the maritime museum at Pickering Park. He had at various times used the models and collections as source material in his work and helped the museum director catalogue the contents more accurately.

It was in 1971 however that Rodmell's long connection with the museum was marked in a very special way when he decided to donate the vast accummulation of

*104. The S.S. **Columbus**, Norddeutscher Lloyd (24 x 37 in.); H. H. Rodmell, 1924. (Town Docks Museum).*

*105. The diesel electric trawler **Cape Trafalgar** (28 x 36 in.); H. H. Rodmell, 1957. (Private Collection).*

106. Royal occasion (26 x 33$^1/_2$ in.); H. H. Rodmell, 1969, the artist's diploma piece for the RSMA. (Hull Museums and Art Gallery).

142

shipping publicity material which had gathered in his studio at Hornsea amounting to over seven hundred items. This collection which the donor asked to be named the Hudson Rodmell bequest, includes the original illustrations for the *Lookout Man*, many of the pen drawings of the 'Humber Traders' series, gouache studies for posters and the final printed versions as well as numerous handbills, brochures and calendars. [258]

This is a remarkable assemblage and highly instructive to the student of British poster art and its evolution in the inter-war period. Two years later in 1973 he gave a collection of some ten thousand ship photographs, cuttings and reproductions to the National Maritime Museum at Greenwich. This stemmed from his earliest childhood interest in the sea and had developed into an invaluable source of reference during his long career. The National Maritime Museum also owns 'Gale Force 8', an oil painting of a Hull trawler in heavy weather which was hung in the 1964 RSMA exhibition and given by the society. They also have as part of their diploma a collection of pictures by members of the Royal Society of Marine Artists, a study entitled 'Royal Occasion'. Originally shown at the Ferens in 1970 it depicts the royal yacht *Britannia* in the King George Dock, Hull, with HMS *Malcolm* in attendance.*

His health declined over the ensuing years but he still sent pictures to the annual exhibition of local artists at the Ferens Art Gallery and the shows held by the Friends of Beverley Minster. In 1976 he painted an acrylic of trawlers in the Princes Dock for the new fishing gallery at the Town Docks Museum. Unfortunately he was unable to attend the official opening and he never was able to visit the new establishment which would have been a surprising contrast to the Aladdin's cave jumble of the old fisheries museum he had known so well. Probably his last important commission was an invitation by the Royal Insititute of Painters in watercolour to contribute to an album of drawings which was presented as a wedding gift to Prince Charles and Lady Diana Spencer in 1981.

Harry Hudson Rodmell died on 3 March 1984, a great loss to his family and friends and all those who have enjoyed his pictures throughout a long working life. Harry Rodmell was a commercial artist of great profesional skill and one of the outstanding poster makers of his generation. He was also a first class watercolourist and an artist in the full sense of that word. He was constantly developing and eagerly embraced new materials, finding acrylic a medium which suited the looser style of his mature years. The finely detailed ship portraits were abandoned in favour of imaginative studies created from memory and his sketch book jottings. At the very end of his career he produced a number of abstracts which are the logical conclusion of his increasingly free approach to painting but for a man in his late seventies are remarkable for their vivid colour and sheer verve. An oil painting of a trawler, battling through fiercely raging seas which he called 'Storm Force 10' was begun whilst in his eighties. It remained unfinished at his death and now hangs in the sitting room of his home at Hornsea.

Sadly the exhibition held at the Town Docks Museum, 24th August - 23rd September 1984 had to be a posthumous tribute to the artist. Originally it had been intended as a retrospective and the first major one-man show of his long career. Since that time his work has become increasingly well-known especially with the renewed interest in poster art. Examples of his work in this field were shown in Rotterdam in 1987 in an exhibition entitled *Schip end Affiche* shown at the Prins Hendrick Museum.

* The diploma collection was transferred from Greenwich to Hull Museums and Art Gallery in 1991.

ALLANSON HICK (1898-1975)

Allanson Hick was born on 19 June 1898 at 89 Walton Street, Hull (fig. 107). [259] His father was a mariner, a captain with Hull's Wilson Line and his mother also came from a seafaring family. Their relatives the Boxall family were neighbours and John Boxall was fourth officer on the ill-fated *Titanic*. This background and an evident love of ships might seem to have made a career in the merchant navy inevitable. Instead however of entering the Hull Trinity House Navigation School he became an architect pupil in the office of Wheatley and Houldsworth at the age of sixteen. This was 1914 and following the outbreak of war he answered Kitchener's call for volunteers, though against his parent's wishes and under age. He saw service with the East Yorkshire Regiment in the Near East and on the Western Front and latterly, probably after the armistice, was transferred or attached to the Royal Scots Regiment. While in Scotland he met Sarah Knight McCowan, always known as Sadie, and they eventually married in Perth on 17 April 1926, when she was 25 and Hick was 28. They settled in Hull where he resumed his professional career as an architectural assistant with Wheatley and Houldsworth before moving to the larger practice of Gelder and Kitchen.

The earliest dated works by Hick are a handful of postcard size sketches produced in Scotland during and immediately after the war but a flow of accomplished drawings and paintings only really began in the 1930's. He was a member of the Hull Atelier of Architects, founded in 1921, an organisation which had regular meetings at the local Metropole Hotel but later transferred its activities to the Hull College of Art. Hick's skills as a draughtsman developed considerably and his early domestic and commercial work included new offices for the Dundee, Perth and London Shipping Co. in 1928 while an assistant in the office of W. B. Blanchard. By now he was holder of a licentiate of the Royal Institute of British Architects and was not finding the mixed practice, which included an estate agency, congenial to his tastes. In 1930 Hick's partnership began with G. Dudley Harbron, then aged 50, a man of considerable intellect, an author, regular contributor to the *Architects Journal*, lecturer at the local school of architecture, with a long record of professional practice. The younger man now had more freedom to follow his own inclinations and in a period of economic depression when business was slack he had plenty of time to draw and paint. Hick had a great appreciation for the work of Muirhead Bone (1876-1953) who displayed a phenomenal talent for draughtsmanship. William Walcot (1874-1943) an architect and graphic artist, whose drawings and engravings are only now beginning to receive due recognition again, was another early hero. Claude Muncaster (1903-74) was also a great favourite and this artist's splendid studies of deck scenes aboard sailing vessels must have held a particular appeal. Muncaster had practical experience under sail including a spell in the four-masted bark *Olivebank* one of Gustav Erikson's grain ships sailing out of Mariehamn in the Baltic.

Allanson Hick was able to build up his own small but well-chosen collection of pictures which also included work by Gemmell Hutchison (1853-1936), the Scots genre painter, and Ann Redpath (1895-1965) painter of landscape and still-life, a now much acclaimed representative of the Scottish school. Philip Connard (1975-1958), also represented in his collection, was a painter and designer who was well known for his murals aboard the RMS *Queen Mary*. He also provided some miniature murals for Queen Mary's doll's house at Windsor!

Allanson Hick's skills and technique matured until in 1935 he had three works accepted for the Royal Academy exhibition, including a watercolour study of

108. *Four-masted bark **Parma** of Mariehamn ($13^1/_2$ x $15^1/_2$ in.); Allanson Hick, c.1935, a watercolour. (Town Docks Museum).*

*109. The destroyer **Onslaught** (13$^1/_4$ x 18 in.); Allanson Hick, 1944, a watercolour. (Town Docks Museum).*

the four-masted bark *Pommern*. This was another of Erikson's grain ships, which the artist had seen in Hull and which in 1939 was the last full-rigged ship to sail out of the port. Other sailing ships which took his eye were the *Pamir* and *Passat*, the *Olivebank* and *Viking* which were all working vessels earning their keep as traders (fig. 108 and pl. 50). He found a fellow enthusiast for these beautiful sailing craft in Harry Cartidge, a local photographer of note, and they often hitched a ride on a tug or a tender to observe these vessels as they were towed up or down the Humber. Hick regularly exhibited at the Academy until 1955 and threequarters of the works were marine subjects but it was structure which attracted him, the bare poles and yards, the shape of a ships hull rather than the romantic allure of billowing canvas or ocean liners in exotic locations. He loved to draw masts and cranes and there are fine studies of Castle Howard and York Minster dressed in scaffolding. In 1935 he drew his first calendar for the insurance brokers Richards, Hibbert and Co. and this became a regular commission until 1973, shortly before his death. Usually executed in pen and ink the subjects were mainly architectural such as the Hull City Hall, Beverley Minster, Patrington Church but also included a view of the Hull-New Holland ferry, seen through the framework of the pier, and the continental car ferry at King George Dock.

Hick's great friend and fellow ship lover was Harry Hudson Rodmell (1896-1984) a notable marine painter and one of the great designers of shipping posters in the inter-war period. In 1936 both men were elected to the Society of Graphic Artists and the two of them were founder members of the Society of Marine Artists a body initiated by Charles Pears, the first president, and a fellow Yorkshireman. The inaugural exhibition planned for October 1939 was cancelled owing to the outbreak of war but both Hick and Rodmell contributed to the United Artists exhibition at Burlington House and the Royal Academy exhibition of 1940, included two works by Hick, 'Dory depots' and 'Seven for Tomorrow'.

He applied for a position as an offical war artist and though this privilege was denied to him he did gain permission to make drawings anywhere within the Humber defences. Hick clearly took advantage of the opportunity and the artist has left us a unique record of the repair and refitting of warships and auxiliaries in the Hull docks during the war. Cameras were strictly forbidden in this restricted zone but Hick was able to reproduce in his drawings all the ships externals including armaments and any outward signs of the top secret radar and direction-finding equipment. Most of the sheets bear marks of the censors pencil and stamps on the reverse, either forbidding their publication at the time or making it conditional on the deletion of sensitive details such as ships serial numbers, radio aerials and any indication of location (fig. 109). On one occasion at least, in November 1944, he was able to hitch a ride on a destroyer, the *Onslaught*, while it was undergoing trials after a major refit and he has given us a series of rapid sketches made above and below decks. Most if not all of these studies remained unpublished until the cessation of hostilities but in 1946 '*Onslaughts new shaft*' formed the subject of his diploma piece for the (Royal) Society of Marine Artists. A pen and wash version was shown at the Royal Academy in 1948 and another variant was hung at the RSMA exhibition so late as 1972.

The favourite haunt of the artist and his friends and acquaintances was Jenny's cafe. This was run by his sister-in-law Jenny Chamberlain and occupied the basement of two Georgian terrace houses at 3-4 Bond Street, which Hick had converted in 1936. He and Harbron established their office on the first floor and the remainder was let as flats. His designs for the cafe included not only the building work but the furniture and fittings too, tables and chairs in lined oak, blue-grey folk weave curtains and upholstery, decor in pale buff and dull blue and the carved and embossed stone slab bearing the blue coffee pot sign at the entrance. Other habitues were members of the repertory company who performed at the nearby Little Theatre and the Hull Art Club, founded in 1932, made Jenny's Cafe their headquarters which quickly established itself as the city's informal centre for the arts. Although damaged in the blitz it continued to function surrounded by debris and propped up by heavy timbers. During 1942 Hick found time to lecture at the Hull School of Architecture although the frequent attentions of the German bombers caused him and his wife to move to Hornsea where his old friend Harry Rodmell was already established.

Both he and Harbron, his partner, had strong characters and it was perhaps inevitable that the association should be dissolved in 1949. He described himself in the following terms. 'It is generally known that I have a somewhat excitable nature and can be relied upon to warm up readily, even to explosive condition, and indulge in the most provoking statements especially if the subject is one about which I have intense feelings!'

Allanson Hick's office became more like a painter's studio and less like an architect's office until in 1961 the Bond Street premises were compulsorily purchased and the much loved Jenny's cafe was closed forever. In 1954-5 he was president of the prestigious York and East Yorkshire Architectural Society and in 1958 was elected a member of the Art Workers Guild. He died in the Hull Royal Infirmary, 11 May 1975, and the artist's diploma piece was displayed at the annual exhibition of the RSMA that year as a tribute to his memory.

The largest single group of his pictures to appear in the sale rooms was at Leeds in 1988 and the fourteen lots had as the star item the bark *Pommern* his academy piece of 1935.

COLIN VERITY (b. 1924)

Born on 7 March 1924 in Darwen, Lancs., he was educated at Malet Lambert High School, Hull, with additional private tuition. For four out of five years he was awarded the form prize for art and handicrafts. From an early age it was aviation that he found engrossing and it was his intention after matriculation to enter the R.A.F. College, Cranwell, and after ten years service to transfer to a commercial airline as a pilot, but the outbreak of the 1939-45 war put paid to that idea. Instead when he became of military age Verity volunteered and was accepted in the RAF but placed on deferred service awaiting call up. Prior to this he had commenced architectural studies at the Hull School of Architecture interrupted by his eventual entry for pilot training. Demobilised on the B release scheme in 1946 to return to his architectural course he joined the Hull City Architects department two years later. Verity remained with them, except for a brief period in private practice with the Hull firm of Gelder and Kitchen, until local government reorganisation in 1974 when he moved to the Humberside County Architects department. After ten years as principal architect he took early retirement in 1984 to devote his time to painting (fig. 110).

The first painting of which he has any recollection, and which he still possesses, was created (according to his late father's note) at the age of four. The subject was the Blue Star Liner, *Arandora Star* which was moored in Gladstone Dock, Liverpool, opposite the Cunard Liner *Franconia*. His father had taken him on a visit to the *Franconia* on a public open day, and on returning home he produced the painting from memory on brown wrapping paper.

In parallel with painting as a hobby he also had an obsession for model building - particularly aircraft both flying and non-flying exhibition scale as well as ships and the American steam railway which he modelled to a scale of 3.2mm - 1 foot. (HO. scale).

He won many prizes and awards locally and nationally. Models were built for the Admiralty and the Air Ministry and architectural models for numerous bodies including the City Architects, Humberside County Council, Gelder and Kitchen, the Docks Board, Gilstrap Earp and Co. Ltd. and Associated British Maltsters. Models were to various scales depending on the project the largest ever being twelve feet by seven feet and the largest ship model eight feet long.

Painting until the mid-sixties was a limited activity with works shown annually at the Ferens Local Artists Exhibition, later to become known as the Ferens Winter Exhibition. Then he began to paint on a more regular basis, the subjects being shipping and the American and British steam railway with a smattering of traction engines and aircraft. Verity's first major commission was a large oil painting of express locomotives standing ready for the road at the King's Cross engine shed, for a museum in Warwick. In the early 1970's an association began which still continues with the Francis Iles Gallery in Rochester, Kent, who wanted as many shipping and railway paintings as he could supply and many commissions originated through this gallery. It was Francis Iles who first submitted his marine paintings to the annual exhibition of the Royal Society of Marine Artists and two years later in 1974 he was invited to become a member. The annual exhibitions produced many sales and commissions, three paintings being purchased by the National Maritime Museum at Greenwich for the Nation's permanent collection. They were: 'Trawlers abreast - St. Andrews Dock', 'The *Clan Malcolm* in King George dock, Hull' and the 'Spurn Lightship - dry docked in Alexandra dock'.

Further commissions followed through the Federation of British Artists notable among which have been a series of paintings for the Sultanate of Oman and Lloyds of London (Aviation).

149

As a member of the R.S.M.A. he has served a number of times as a Council Member of the Society and has on many occasions served on the selection and hanging Committees both for the Annual Exhibition and the exhibitions at the Earl's Court Boat Show. He is also a member of the exclusive Fylingdales Group of Artists, a founder member and president of the Hornsea Art Society, as well as a member of the Guild of Aviation Artists. He remains a regular exhibitor at the R.S.M.A., Earls Court Boat Show, The Ferens Art Gallery, Beverley Art Gallery, Francis Iles Gallery (Rochester), Oliver Swann Gallery, Solent Gallery, Llewellyn Alexander Gallery and numerous other commercial galleries in the U.K. and also supports local charity exhibitions, i.e. the Missions to Seamen, The R.N.L.I. (Whitby) and the Sailors Families Society (figs. 111-2).

In 1982 he was invited to submit works to the Mystic Maritime Gallery at the Mystic Seaport Museum in Connecticut, U.S.A. for the 3rd International Maritime Art Awards exhibition and at that and subsequent exhibitions has been awarded two oil painting and one watercolour painting prizes. As a result of his success the Mystic Gallery gave him an open invitation to submit works without selection to their two major annual exhibitions, The Mystic International and the 'Mystic One Hundred' the latter being work of a selected hundred marine artist from all over the world. His work has also been displayed in Vancouver, Seattle, Boston and Philadelphia.

At the time of writing his paintings are in private, public and corporate collections in sixteen countries including the Sultanate of Oman, P. & O. Line, Ben Line, Harrison Line, Blue Funnel Line, Scandinavian Seaways, Brittany Ferries, Everard Shipping Co., the Kassos Steam Navigation Co. of Greece, The Duke of Gloucester, Shell Tankers, Town Docks Museum, Hull, Humberside Libraries, Gillingham Libraries, Harrogate Gallery and the White Fish Authority.

His paintings have been reproduced as facsimile copies by the P. & O. Line, and as limited edition prints, calendars, greeting and postcards.

The artist frequently demonstrates his painting techniques to art societies and clubs in various parts of the country and has been involved in teaching watercolour painting over a ten year period. He has tutored week and weekend courses to art societies and was a tutor with the 'Galleon Art Holidays' now known as 'Artscape painting Holidays'.

Colin Verity is self-taught having had no formal art training apart from that associated with his training as architect. The marine scene in general provides his main painting subjects with emphasis on the steam and motorship, both merchant and naval of the 19th and 20th centuries, though not to the exclusion of the great age of sail painted mainly for the American market. He believes that marine painting should not be undertaken without careful study and analysis of the structure and working of the ship. Knowledge, and careful observation with an ability to draw are an essential part of marine painting, for ships are very unforgiving to the indifferent draughtsman and no amount of 'Arty Verbosity' can camouflage this fact. Paintings of ships at sea are essentially a close relationship between a meteorological situation and its reaction on a ship in other words the sky determines the sea state to which the ship reacts. The Hull docks, a meeting point of all types of ships and associated activities have always been a source of subject matter and inspiration.

The majority of his painting time is taken up with commissioned work which he looks upon as a challenge and invariably involves a considerable amount of research particularly if it is a nautical event being recorded. He is quite often asked to paint a ship that no longer exists which means searching for as many photographs as can be found to build up a feeling for the ship in question, or, better still the acquisition of the general arrangement drawings of the ship.

His architectural experience enables him to look at the drawings and see a ship in three dimensions, not a series of lines on a piece of paper. He is then able to produce a series of sketches to select the most appropriate angle from which to view the ship to bring out its individual features, rather like painting a portrait in a a

110. Colin Verity.

*111. 'Steamers at low
tide' (18 x 24 in.).
Private collection;
Colin Verity, 1980.*

way, since every ship like every person is unique.

He is currently (1991) engaged in producing a series of paintings showing the development of the Kassos Steam Navigation Co. of Greece, a company which has its origins in the late eighteenth century. He is also engaged in speculative paintings for a number of exhibitions the two most important being the 'Mystic International' USA and the R.S.M.A. Annual Exhibition in London. (pl. 52-54).

*112. 'Vital maintenance', trawler **Loch Inver** in dry dock (26 x 48 in.). Private collection; Colin Verity, 1981.*

J. STEVEN DEWS (b. 1949)

Born in Beverley his grandfather was assistant dockmaster in Hull but his own nautical ambitions were thwarted by failure to gain a place in either the Trinity House School or the Boulevard Nautical College. He has however subsequently established himself as a skilled yachtsman and has cruised extensively along the coast of Britain and has done a spell as a watch officer aboard the *Winston Churchill*, the Hessle built schooner of the Sail Training Association. In his 36ft. yacht *Fine Art* Dews won first prize in the Winter Series of the Portsmouth Division Races of 1989 (fig. 113). [260]

At the Hull Regional College of Art he transferred from the fine arts course to graphics but was determined to establish himself as a marine artist. After supporting himself with numerous temporary jobs he set up a studio in a derelict farmhouse in Sunk Island maintaining himself with part-time illustration while working hard at his oil painting. An association with James Starkey the Beverley gallery owner began in 1973 and led to his first one-man exhibition three years later which was a sell-out and led to a host of new commissions. [261] In 1977 Steven was able to spend several days aboard the United Towing vessel *Winchman* in the North Sea which resulted in 'Winchman at work with the barge *Champion* in the Ekofisk field' and *Lloydsman* towing the jack-up rig Al Ghallan. [262] A commission for a painting of the coasting vessel *Alice P.G.* built at the Yorkshire Dry Dock Company's yard in Hull was delivered in 1978 to Mrs. Mary Smyth, wife of Ron Smyth the racehorse trainer, who had launched the vessel. [263] After another sell-out exhibition in San Francisco he was asked by the curator of the San Francisco Maritime Museum for a painting of the four-masted bark *Star of Poland* built in 1901 and wrecked in 1918 on the coast of Japan.

In 1980 AMOCO commissioned him to paint a series of twelve subjects for their calendar and these were issued as limited edition prints illustrating famous British Ships from Drake's the *Golden Hind* to Naomi James' yacht the *Express Crusader*. [264]

Money raised from the sale of the prints was given to the trust set up to raise the sixteenth century warship *Mary Rose* and undertake its conservation and display.

Other similar projects were undertaken for B.P. and the Woolwich Building Society and a set of seven paintings were produced for Peter Lowell managing director of Brekkes Ltd., the Hull fish processing firm, to celebrate their centenary, 1880-1980. These include a variety of trawlers from the *Imperial Queen* to a Boyd line vessel of the 1930's. A large canvas of the St. Andrews dock extension has the S.T. *Lord Tedder* in the foreground.

In the aftermath of the Falklands Campaign he was asked to paint the M.V. *Norland* the Hull-Rotterdam ferry which had been requisitioned for troop carrying. The picture was presented in 1983 to Don Ellerby, her master, who commanded the vessel in the North Sea and on active service in the South Atlantic. [265]

The artist gave a painting of the *Earl of Pembroke*, the vessel which became Cooks' *Endeavour*, to be auctioned by Christies in aid of the RNLI in 1984. It was a gift he was happy to make as repayment for the help he received from the local lifeboat when he got into difficulties off Lowestoft. [266] In 1986 Dews was asked to be the offical marine artist to the America Cup British Challenge Team. [267] Two of the originals subsequently fetched substantial prices in the London salerooms [268] and the Marine Galleries at Cowes offered for sale limited edition prints of the 'White Crusader versus USA,' 'New Zealand versus Stars and Stripes' and 'Stars and Stripes versus Kookaburra.'

In 1985 the same gallery had published a limited edition of 'J Class - 1934' and availabe in 1987 were open editions of the yacht 'America' and the 'Rainbow

and *Endeavour*' as well as limited editions of '*Sceptre* and *Evaine* 1958' and '*Britannia* racing off Cowes.'

For the Australian Bicentennial celebrations in 1988 he was commissioned by the New South Wales Services Board to produce two pictures, of the First Fleet reenactment and the accompanying assembly of tall ships. This also led to a private order for another version of this subject. [269]

Limited edition prints followed of the S.T.S. *Winston Churchill* and the 'Whaler *Phoenix* off Greenwich, 1820', published by Felix Rosenstiels's Widow and Son of London (pl. 55). The latter work was inspired by a decorated whale's tooth of the London whaleship *Phoenix* displayed in the Town Docks Museum, Hull. Further Rosenstiel prints were published in 1990 of '8 metres racing off West Solent' and '*Candida* and *Astra* off Cowes' (pl. 56) [270]

Probably the artists most unusual production was the pair of shoes with painted soles which were sold at auction by Bonhams, 10 August 1989. One has yachts off Dover and the other a fishing boat. [271]

A clear statement of the artist's approach to painting and his technique was recently published in a magazine article and it is well worth reprinting an extract from this:

'I work from detailed reference books, ships and models and architectural drawings together with my library of photographs and begin producing several small sketches to outline the composition. I then do several more small drawings incorporating detailed measurements and calculations to ensure accuracies of scale. This is most imporant in creating paintings which are to be viewed by critical marine enthusiasts. At this stage I have an idea in my mind of the mood I wish to create. I then produce a detailed, highly finished pencil drawing approximately, 10 x 12 ins. which, in addition to giving the client a better idea of how the finished painting will look, gives me an opportunity to see how much detail can satisfactorily be fitted in the composition.

I buy professionally made stretcher pieces and high quality linen canvas, already primed from Bird and Davis, which I sand down and often re-prime with an oil based primer to further improve the ground and body of the painting. I then sketch in the chosen subject matter with a soft pencil directly onto the primed base. Next, I paint over the whole canvas using a flat brush, turps and burnt sienna. This is followed by painting the sky and filling in the sea area usually favouring the horizon placed at a measured third from the bottom of the canvas. I complete the sky first and then block in the main subject matter. After this I turn my attention to the sea. It is this correct combination and balance between the sky and sea which is most important in determining the mood of the painting. I must, of course, make accurate judgements of weather conditions and the effect they have on the interaction of these elements. I then work on the main subject matter building up the layers of paint by using a quick drying liquid.' [272]

Steven Dews work is in terrific demand and he currently produces some ten to twelve large canvases a year . This means that there is a lengthy waiting list for new commissions though the print editions help to provide eager buyers with examples of his art. [273] Currently he is preparing material for an exhibition at the Windjammer Gallery in Bermuda to be held in Autumn 1992. Earlier in 1991 he was making preparatory notes and sketches for this during Bermuda Yachting Race Week. [274] Steven however still has his home in East Yorkshire where he lives with his wife Mary and two children.

DAVID BELL (b. 1950)

Born at Goxhill, Lincs., in 1950 he came to Hull at the age of fourteen to begin three years training at the Trinity House Navigation School. During this time painting was his main hobby and he won a number of prizes for his artwork. These early impressions of the port of Hull and the influence of the school with its long history steeped in maritime tradition provided inspiration for many of his paintings. At seventeen he joined the merchant navy as a navigator and spent the next eight years gaining first hand experience of the oceans of the world, from the Northern seas (including a voyage in the trawler *St. Loman*) to the South Seas in a tanker. Much as he loved the life at sea his abiding passion was for painting and drawing and he decided to come ashore. Bell began a three year design course at the Hull College of Art where he was able to experiment with various techniques and media, eventually gaining an honours degree, appropriately enough submitting a dissertation on the Hull marine artists of the nineteenth and twentieth centuries. During this period he moved from a meticulous style using ink and wash to a looser technique relying for its effect on the interplay of light and shade and the use of soft washes of colour (fig. 114).

Living and working in Hull he took his subjects from the locality and featured the traditional craft of the Humber, the keels and sloops, and vessels of the city's great trawler fleet. In 1981 a local printing company, Meridian Masters, commissioned several pictures of river scenes and as the Humber Bridge was under construction he decided to paint a scene depicting the old and the new. [275] The paddle steamer *Lincoln Castle* was depicted passing beneath the bridge - a piece of artistic licence, since by the time the bridge was finished she had gone out of service. Entitled 'Humber Heritage' it proved a very popular print and the original was presented to Her Majesty the Queen at the official opening of the bridge in 1984.

The same year, two years after the Falkland campaign, Bell received a commission from, the army [276] to record the FIPASS (Falkland Island Port and Storage System) pontoon a huge floating facility for the troops stationed in the South Atlantic. He was flown out to Port Stanley to make on the spot sketches and in the event spent some time with each of the services including three days on HMS *Penelope* working in and around San Carlos Sound. During his stay further commissions were received from the Royal Scots at Goose Green as well as the Royal Engineers, R.A.F. and R.E.M.E. and during his time in the Falklands he completed many island landscapes. His experiences of his visit enabled Bell to develop his repertoire and combine landscapes and marine subjects with increasing skill.

On his return the Kingston Engraving Co. asked him to paint the *Norland* in San Carlos Sound to raise money for the South Atlantic Fund. [277] The *Norland* was a local vessel, a ro-ro ferry in the Hull-Rotterdam service which had been requisitioned during the conflict in the South Atlantic.

A painting of the *Northella* and *Junella* two Hull stern trawlers requisitioned by the navy for use in the Falklands campaign was presented to Capt. Jeremy Stuart in 1983. [278] He also painted the *Sir Walter Raleigh* a Hull trawler converted for use as the Operation Raleigh support ship and a print of this was sold to raise funds for the expedition. [279]

An ongoing relationship with Parker Polymers has produced a series of commissions of RNLI lifeboats, all of which have been issued in print form and have been significant fund raisers for the institution. The pictures include the lifeboats of Spurn, Guernsey, Alderney and Bridlington; painted in oil they have translated admirably into prints without losing any of their detail and clarity. Indeed they amply testify to the dramatic appeal and

*114. David Bell in his
studio, 1987.*

*115. HMS **Victory** from
'Britains Maritime
History' 1982 (8$^1/_4$ x 11
in.); D. C. Bell.*

H.M.S. *VICTORY*

interest which can be captured in an artistic production as opposed to a photograph.

A splendid showcase for Bell's work was the book published in 1982, entitled *Britains Maritime History* a limited edition of three hundred copies handsomely bound in leather. Line drawings and a series of twelve subjects hand coloured by the artist illustrate a variety of craft from Elizabethan galleons to modern warships accompanied by a text also supplied by David Bell (fig. 115).

A one-man show of watercolours, and lithographs was given at the James Starkey Galleries, Beverley in December 1985 and three years later a collection of oils was shown there, fifteen subjects including sailing ships, trawlers and the Humber ferry. [280]

He has also had shows in Hull, Ireland and Canada and his work has been included in prestigious London exhibitions. He has now returned to his native Lincolnshire where he lives with his wife and four children but still maintains strong ties with Hull which he visits frequently (pls. 58-9). [281]

*1. Anon. 'HMS **Hector**, 1743' (31 x 50 in.), Town Docks Museum; a fifth rate of 44 guns launched at Hugh Blaydes shipyard Hessle Cliff, a site at what is now the northern landfall of the Humber Bridge.*

2. Robert Thew (attributed) 'West end of the New Dock at Hull' ($12^3/_8$ x $20^1/_2$ in.), Ferens Art Gallery; this subject and its companion piece were issued as prints in 1786. The dock was opened in 1778 and named Queens Dock after the visit of Queen Victoria and Prince Albert in 1854. It was filled in, commencing 1930, and is now represented by the Queen Gardens.

3. Anon. 'The Standidge fleet, 1769, ($12^3/_8$ x $20^1/_2$), Ferens Art Gallery; probably painted in 1788 it derives from the print published in 1754 which was based on Charles Brooking's 'Greenland

4. Anon. 'The steam packet **Royal Charter** at Barton Waterside' (33 x 43 in.), Town Docks Museum. A naive painting c.1820.

5. George Chambers (1803-40) 'The port of Hull with the brig **Spartan** in two views' (31 x 46 in.) Ferens Art Gallery; signed and dated 1827. The vessel was built at Whitby in 1826 by Thomas Brodrick for John Brodrick, a Hull merchant whose descendant Cuthbert achieved fame as architect of the Leeds Town Hall, Hull Royal Institution, etc.

6. *John Wilson Carmichael (1759-1869), 'The shipyard at Hessle Cliffs' (34 x 47$\frac{1}{4}$ in.) Ferens Art Gallery; signed and dated 1829. The yard passed through the hands of John Frame, Hugh Blaydes, a Mr. Hodgson and from c.1815 to its closure was owned by Barkworth and Hawkes.*

7. Anon. 'The tugs **Hecla** and **Lightning** off Victoria Pier' 21 x 35$^{1}/_{2}$in.) Town Docks Museum; these vessels built 1860 and 1865 respectively belonged to Thomas and John Gray of Hull. Executed with precision these two tugs might well have been painted directly from the general arrangement drawings of the builder.

10. Robert Willoughby 'The whaling ship **Ocean, 1817**' (24 x 36 in.), private collection; built at Yarmouth in 1812 the vessel sailed in the Arctic fishery under the ownership of James Hewetson, a Hull merchant, until 1819 when she was lost at Davis Strait.

163

8. Thomas Fletcher, 'The **Molly** and **Friends**' (39 x 54 in.) Town Docks Museum; the whaleboats in the foreground bear the initials A.S. of Angus Sadler, master of the **Molly** between 1796 and 1802.

9. Robert Willoughby 'The Cooper fleet, 1803' (53 x 70 in.) Town Docks Museum; signed and dated 1 April 1803 it depicts the whaling fleet of Samuel Cooper a Hull merchant; from left to right each shown in two views: **Thomas**, stern view and profile; **Brothers**, ditto; **Samuel**, ditto; **North Briton**, ditto.

11. Robert Willoughby, 'The house of William Westerdale, mast, block and pump maker, 1 Pier Street', Hull Museums; this shows the newly made Hull waterfront built up from the spoil excavated from the Humber dock which opened to shipping in 1809.

13. Binks and Griffin 'The paddle steamers **Kingston, Prince Frederick,** and **Calder**' (20 x 40 in.) Ferens Art Gallery; the **Prince Frederick**, built 1823 and **Kingston**, built 1821, belonged to the Hull Steam Packet Co.; the Calder was a river steamer of the Aire and Calder Navigation Co. The vessels were almost certainly painted by Griffin and the sea and sky by Binks.

12. William Barton 'A baltic brig in two views, off Paull,1810 (26 x 36 in.) Ferens Art Gallery; Hull can be seen on the horizon and Humber Keels with their characteristic square sails.

14. Thomas Binks 'The whaleships **Jane, Viewforth** and **Middleton** beset in the Arctic, 1835' (25 x 36 in.) Town Docks Museum; signed and dated 1836. The **Jane** of Hull is in the centre of the picture, the **Viewforth** of Kirkcaldy and the **Middleton** of Aberdeen on either side.

16. William Griffin 'The Whaleship **Jane**, with the **Harmony,** off Hull'; signed and dated 1837. Probably painted to celebrate the end of the **Jane**'s whaling career and the survival of both vessels from the severe conditions of the 1836 season. (Private Collection).

15. *William Griffin 'The Whaleship **Mary Frances'** (24 x 39$^1/_2$) Town Docks Museum; commissioned by Captain William Couldrey to celebrate a bumper catch of whales in 1832.*

17. William Griffin 'The paddle steamers **Rob Roy, Emperor** and **Queen of Scotland** (19$^1/_2$ x 36 in.) Town Docks Museum; all three vessels belonged to Joseph Gee and Co; the **Rob Roy** built for them in 1836, the **Emperor** in 1848 and the **Queen of Scotland** purchased in 1843.

18. Reuben Griffin 'The Confederate raider **Alabama** and the **Kearsage,** of the Federal navy, engaged off Cherbourg in 1864' (26 x 36 in.) Town Docks Museum; the **Alabama,** on the right, was sunk and survivors were taken aboard the S.Y. **Deerhound** (centre).

*19. John Ward, 'The **William Lee** in the Arctic' (27 x 39 in.) Town Docks Museum; commissioned by Richard Hill, her captain in 1831 or 1832.*

20. John Ward 'The paddle steamer *Victoria*' (23 x 35 in.) Hull Trinity House; built in 1837 for the Hull Steam Packet Co., she was lost in 1853.

21. John Ward 'A riverside caprice' (11 x 19 in.) Town Docks Museum; a panel painting.

*22. John Ward 'The paddle steamer **Wilberforce**' (18 x 24 in.) Town Docks Museum; an engraving after an oil painting, now lost. Published in 1838 to celebrate the vessel's entry into service for the Humber Union Steam Packet Co.*

*23. John Ward 'The **Swan** and **Isabella**' (13 x 20 in.) Town Docks Museum; the **Swan** on the left, sailed in the Hull whaling fleet from 1824-1840 and the **Isabella** from 1824 until 1835 when she was crushed in the pack ice of Davis Strait.*

*24. John Ward 'The brig **Helen**' (24 x 35 in.) Ferens Art Gallery; built at Sutton in 1837 by William Gibson for William Priest and William Lambert of Hull who put her in the Baltic trade.*

174

*25. John Ward 'The paddle steamer **Waterwitch'** (9 x 12 in.) Town Docks Museum; painted on panel. Built in 1836 for the Humber Union Steam Packet Co. she was sold in 1841 to the General Steam Navigation Co. of London.*

*28. William Ward 'The whaleship **Truelove'** (19 x 24$^1/_2$) Town Docks Museum; watercolour signed and dated 1801. She entered the Hull whaling fleet in 1784 and made her last voyage to the fishery in 1868, a total of 72 seasons in the Arctic.*

26. John Ward 'The return of the **William Lee'** (24 x 36 in.) Ferens Art Gallery; the vessel is depicted entering the Humber dock basin 22 January, 1839, after a voyage to Calcutta. She was managed by Joseph Gee for Thomas Thompson and George Liddell, a Hull banker.

*27a. John Ward 'HMS **Britannia**, port side stern view'; (13 x 9 in.)*
Town Docks Museum; a lithographic print, hand coloured.
*The **Britannia**, a first rate man-of-war of 120 guns, became a cadet training vessel in 1859.*

*27b. John Ward 'HMS **Britannia** starboard side, stern view' (13 x 9 in.)
Town Docks Museum; a lithographic print, hand coloured.*

29. W. F. Settle 'A brig moored at the dolphin off the South Blockhouse' (7$^1/_2$ x 13 in.) Town Docks Museum; water-colour with some body colour.

30. Henry Redmore 'The wreck of the **Coupland** in Scarborough bay, 2 Nov. 1861' (9$^1/_4$ x 15$^1/_4$ in.). (Private Collection).

31. Henry Redmore 'Hull from the Humber, 1876' (53 x 84 in.) Town Docks Museum.

33. Henry Redmore 'Cobles at Robin Hoods Bay, 1885' (11$^{1}/_{2}$ x 19$^{1}/_{2}$ in.). (Private Collection).

32. Henry Redmore 'Busy morning in Scarborough, 1887' (37 x 62 in.) Town Docks Museum. One of the artist's last major works.

*34. James Wheldon 'The whaleship **Diana** in three views' (24 x 36 in.) Town Docks Museum.*

*36. W. D. Penny, 'The sailing ship **Miranda'** (24 x 36 in.) Town Docks Museum; signed and dated 1866.*

*35. James Wheldon 'An assemblageof shipping' (36 x 82 in.) Town Docks Museum; signed and dated 1872. From left to right; steam yacht **Deerhound**; a Humber sloop and a Dutch hoy; USS **Kearsage**; HMS **Shannon**; C.S. **Alabama**; HMS **Duke of Wellington**; HMS **St. George**; HMS Audacious and HMS **Royal Sovereign**.*

*37. R. D. Widdas, 'The whaleship **Diana** beset in the ice, 1866' (19 x 26 in.) Town Docks Museum; signed and dated 1867.*

*38. S. H. Wilson 'The opening of the Albert dock, 22 July 1869' (22 x 40 in.) Town Docks Museum; signed and dated 1870. The Prince of Wales proceeding through the dock in the royal yacht **Victoria** and **Albert**.*

39. S. H. Wilson 'The steamship **Antelope** in the Humber' (25 x 33 in.) Town Docks Museum; purchased in 1858 by Pearson and Coleman of Hull whose house flag flies from the foremast, she was sunk in 1890 after a collision in the North Sea.

41. Benjamin Tindall, 'The bark **Westa** off Spurn, a pilot cutter in the offing'; the Ålands Museum.

*40. S. H. Wilson 'The S.S. **Oder** and S.S. **Ouse**' (19 x 31 in.) Town Docks Museum; The **Oder** was built at Earles shipyard in 1861 and the **Ouse** the following year in the same yard.*

42. *W. R. Nixon 'The Hull Keel regatta, 1874,* **Kiero** *winning the Bailey and Leetham prize' (23 x 35 in.) Town Docks Museum. The paddlesteamer* **Axholme**, *the mark boat, flies the flag of the Hull Keel Regatta Club.*

43. Thomas Jacques Somerscales 'The S.S. **Immingham'** (20 x 36 in.) Town Docks Museum; signed and dated 1906. This three screw steam turbine vessel was run by the Great Central Railway.

44. Thomas Jacques Somerscales 'Sailing vessels off the coast' (9 x 12 in.) Ferens Art Gallery; signed and dated 1916. Despite the small scale of the canvas the artist captures the broad expanse of the ocean very effectively.

45. Thomas Jacques Somerscales 'The Pier, Hull' (14^1/$_4$ x 20^1/$_4$ in.) Ferens Art Gallery; signed and dated 1922.

46. Joseph Arnold, 'Steam trawler *St. Vincent* of the Red Cross box fleet' (20$\frac{1}{2}$ x 29$\frac{1}{2}$ in.) Town Docks Museum; Gouache, signed and dated 1912. This vessel was built at Beverley by Cook, Welton and Gemmell for the Hull Steam Fishing and Ice Co.

47. Joseph Arnold 'The pilot cutter S.S. *Commander Cawley* (20 x 29$\frac{1}{2}$ in.) Town Docks Museum; Gouache, signed and dated 1914. Built in 1900 for the Humber Pilot Steam Cutter Co. she remained in service until 1931.

48. Harry Hudson Rodmell 'The S.S. **Columbus**' (24 x 37 in.) Town Docks Museum; signed and dated 1924 it was commissioned by Norddeutscher Lloyd owners of the vessel but retrieved by the artist shortly before the war and presented to Hull Museums.

49. Harry Hudson Rodmell 'Southampton-New York,
the Hamburg-America line (25 x 40 in.) Town Docks
Museum; a lithographic poster c.1925.

*50. Allanson Hick 'The four-masted bark **Parma** in Hull, c.1935 (13¹/₂ x 15¹/₂ in.) Town Docks Museum.*

*51. Allanson Hick 'The United Towing tugs **Rifleman** and **Pinky** in dry dock' (13¹/₄ x 12 in.) Town Docks Museum.*

52. The T.S.S. **Gothic** of the Shaw Savill and Albion Line berthing at the King George Dry Dock, Hull, in the 1950's (13 x 18^1/$_2$ in.). Private Collection; watercolour and gouache, Colin Verity, 1986.

54. 'Waiting to transit the Suez canal'. The S.S. **Benares** moored at Port Said (20 x 30 in.). Private Collection; Colin Verity, 1987.

*53. S.S. **Inanda** in the Port of Spain anchorage, Trinidad, in the early 1930's (24 x 36 in.). Private Collection; Colin Verity, 1987.*

55. J. Steven Dews 'The whaler **Phoenix** off Greenwich, 1820' (20 x 29¹/₂ in.). Private Collection; lithographic print.

*56. J. Steven Dews
'**Candida** and **Astra**
racing off Cowes' (24 x
36 in.); 1989. Private
Collection.*

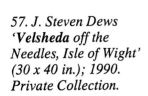

*57. J. Steven Dews
'**Velsheda** off the
Needles, Isle of Wight'
(30 x 40 in.); 1990.
Private Collection.*

58. David Bell 'Hull-New Holland Ferry P.S. **Wingfield Castle**' (14 x 21 in.) Town Docks Museum; a watercolour.

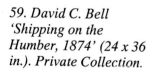

59. David C. Bell 'Shipping on the Humber, 1874' (24 x 36 in.). Private Collection.

A DIRECTORY OF MARINE ARTISTS

The following list includes many names of artists represented only by one or two pictures in the extensive collections of the Town Docks Museum (TDM) or Ferens Art Gallery (FAG). These individuals I am sure in many cases were part-time or amateur painters often seamen who had served on board the particular vessels depicted. Also listed is a sample of the many artists currently working in Hull and district or painting local subjects.

Entries with an asterisk refer to artists described in the main body of the text.

AAR
Crayon drawing of the Wilson line vessel S.S. *Galileo*, signed and dated July 1890 (TDM).

ACP
Oil on board of the smack *Rising Sun* (H.481) signed and dated 1882 (TDM). It was on board this vessel in 1881 that a young apprentice William Papper was murdered by the skipper Osman Brand.

ALLERSTON, John Taylor
Watercolour of HMS *Agincourt*, off Scarborough, signed simply Allerston and dated 1874 (TDM). He lived in Bridlington, a local tradesman who became a professional artist. There are examples of his work in the Bayle Gate Museum, Bridlington.

*(a) Glazed decorated tile (11 x 14 in.); possibly made to commemorate the launch of the **Prince Frederick** for the Hull Steam Packet Co. in 1823. (Town Docks Museum).*

PRINCE FREDRICK of HULL.

APPLEYARD

Oil, signed and dated 1864, of whaleships caught in the ice (TDM).

ARNOLD, Joseph

Painter in gouache on board, primarily of trawlers in the North Sea box fleet and may have been a fisherman himself. A prolific artist but all his recorded works fall within the period 1911-4. From 1895-9 he was living at 50 Portland Street, Hull, and 1900-16 at 1 Cholmley Street. A large number of examples in the TDM and in private hands locally; a picture of the S.T. *Lord Knollys* is in the maritime museum, Esbjerg, Denmark (see pls. 46-7).

ASHTON, J.D. (1875-1942)

An amateur painter he produced some skilful marine works in oil in a nineteenth century style; also Hull townscapes (TDM and FAG). A handsome bone model of a man-of-war by him is displayed in the Town Docks

Museum.

AUSTIN

Watercolour of the S.T. *Lord Hailsham*, signed and dated 1982 (TDM).

BANNISTER, Edward (1821-1916)

Born at 23 Albion Street, 23 September 1821, and apprenticed to John Jacques Matthewson, ornamental painter and fancy chair manufacturer of 9 Junction Street. In July 1864 he set himself up as a portrait painter at number 7, facing Savile Street. Exhibited oils and watercolours at Polytechnic Exhibitions in 1845 and contributed much of the scenery in the basement of the Mechanics Institute for a display called 'The Caverns', 270 ft. in length, decorated with stalactites and torrents, etc. Earlier he had made a series of transparencies for the Zoological Gardens. Subjects, were mainly topographical but with some marines e.g. Burlington Bay (no.94 in 1845). His first attempt at oil painting is

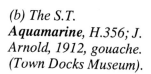

(b) The S.T. Aquamarine, H.356; J. Arnold, 1912, gouache. (Town Docks Museum).

preserved in the Local Studies Library, signed and dated 1841, it shows a Humber Keel at Stoneferry. Brother of Alderman Anthony Bannister J.P., coal merchant and ship owner, he was also a justice of peace.

BARKWORTH, Henry
An oil painting in the National Maritime Museum, Greenwich, depicts a starboard profile view of the Hull-London paddle steamer *Victoria* launched 1837.

* BARTON, William (d.1814)
Panorama painter of Hull who died August 1814.

* BELL, David C. (b.1950)

* BINKS, Thomas (d.1852)

* BINKS, William (d.1842)

BRAY, Alan K. (ARIBA)
Born Hull 30 July 1920, educated at Hull Grammar School and Hull School of Architecture. Articled pupil (1936-40) to Dudley Harbron and Allanson Hick (q.v.). After army service in South-East Asia he became assistant and then partner with Gelder and Kitchen. Drawings in pen and pencil, watercolours, mainly buildings but often combined with river and harbour subjects an inclination formed by his sea-faring family background and association with Hick. One time honorary secretary to the former Hull Art Club. Exhibits locally.

BROOKS, Thomas (1818-92)
Nephew of Thomas Brooks (1770-1840) a carver and gilder of Savile Street, Hull, he was apprenticed to Henry Perronet Briggs RA as was G. P. Green the Hull portrait painter. Painted portraits and genre, a number of the latter with a maritime theme: 'Lifeboat going to the rescue' (RA, 1861); 'Saved from the wreck' (RA 1862); The 'Ebb tide' and the 'Flood tide' (RA 1866); 'Launching the lifeboat' (RA 1868; Ferens Art Gallery permanent collection); 'Wreck in Luscombe Bay' (RA

1869); 'The Missing Boat' (1869); 'A Story of the Sea', 'Thames lilies' (RA 1870); and 'Caught in the gale' (a scene at Runswick) painted in 1870.

There is a a miniature self-portrait in the FAG. See also J. J. Sheahan *History of Kingston upon Hull*, 1866 p.736; *Art Journal*, 1872, p.147-9 which includes a biographical note and engravings of 'Launching the lifeboat', 'The Missing Boat' and 'A Story of the Sea'. At the International Fisheries Exhibition held in London 1883, he exhibited 'Fishing cobles running for shelter, Runswick, Yorkshire' and 'Lynmouth, N. Devon, lifeboat going to the rescue', both offered at £157.10s.0d.

CAIN, T.
Watercolour of the training ship *Southampton*, which was anchored off the mouth of the river Hull from 1867 to 1912 (TDM).

CAMMIDGE, George
Painted landscapes and some pieces of marine interest. An oil of vessels on the Humber bank and another showing the vessel which destroyed the Withernsea pier in 1880 (painted on terracotta) are in private hands. Oils of 'Hollym village' and 'Ghyll Beck, Barden tower' (1878) in FAG. See also illustration dated 1865 'A view of Withernsea, sea front' in Miles and Richardson, *The History of Withernsea*, Hull 1911. A George Cammidge, is recorded as a bricklayer and builder in 1867 and in 1892 as an artist living at Cammidge Street, Withernsea.

CARMICHAEL, R.
Humber pilot and painter in acrylic; reproductions of his canvases of pilot vessels regularly appeared on the Christmas Cards of the Humber Pilots in the 1970's and 1980's.

CHAPPELL, Reuben (1876-1940)
Born in Goole and latterly worked in Cornwall.

CJG
Oil painting of S.S. *Rhine* (TDM).

COBB, J.
Gouache of Wilson Line vessel .s.s. *Borodino* which entered service in 1950 (TDM).

COOK, Peter (b.1944)
Former builder now a professional artist living in his home town of Bridlington. Exhibited at the RSMA from 1977, the Ferens Art Gallery from 1978; a one man show at the Kamarann Studio, Driffield, 1986.

COWLING, G.
Watercolour of the steamship *Harlequin* of Hull, built 1854 and transferred to Sunderland 1871 (TDM).

CRANE, H
Gouache of S.S. *Kasenga* built at Newcastle in 1907 (TDM).

CREDLAND
Oil painting of the bark *Fergus* signed by him in 1939 exhibition at the FAG. This vessel was registered in Hull in 1837 in the ownership of William Blyth, a notable whaling master, and was lost in 1867. The *Hull Rockingham* for 14 May 1831 records the death of Sarah, wife of Thomas Credland, carpenter, Barton-on-Humber.

DAVIES, Roger (b.1945)
Born in Stratford-on-Avon, he attended Newport College of Art 1961-6 and the Royal College of Art 1966-9 where he gained an M.A. Taught at Ulster College of Art 1969-70 and Hull College of Art 1970-1. A watercolourist producing mainly marines and topographical views of the Hull scene.

DAWSON, Henry (1811-78)
Born in Hull 3 April 1811 but his family moved to Nottingham when he was an infant. Apprenticed in lace industry but took lessons from J. B. Pyne and active as an artist in Liverpool after 1844 and London after 1849. Exhibited at the RA; country scenes and coastal views, port scenes. Died at Chiswick 13 December 1878.

(d) Princes Dock, St. John's Church, the Dock Offices and Wilberforce Monument; T. Dudley, 1880. (Private Collection).

* DEWS, J. Steven (b.1949)

DUDLEY, Thomas (fl.1879-1910)
Watercolour artist born in York; in Hull in the 1880's when he painted views of the docks and Old Harbour. Examples of his work are in York City Art Gallery, Victoria and Albert Museum and Wilberforce House, Hull.

EJB
Pair of panel paintings of the Hull paddle-steamers *Vivid* and *Waterwitch*, dated January 1838, are in the Peabody Museum, Salem.

* FLETCHER, Thomas

FORESTER, Maurice
Born in Hull he is a resident in New Zealand; a painting of '*Bounty* running North' depicting the New Zealand built replica of Capt. Bligh's famous vessel - was presented to Prince Charles and Lady Diana Spencer as a wedding present (1981) from the Whangarei City Council. He emigrated in 1962 and for the last few years has worked full time as a marine artist.

FORRESTER, Joseph James
Born in Dundee and was a wine merchant in Hull. He showed two watercolours of the opening of the Junction Dock (Princes Dock), 1 June 1829, along with a chalk drawing of a bust of Apollo in the second exhibition of the Hull and East Riding Institute for the Fine Arts (1829); the former are now in the TDM. He left Hull to become a partner in Offley, Forrester, port wine shippers. (He arrived at Oporto in 1831 and after producing detailed maps of the Douro and the vine district, and a monograph on *Oidium Tuckeri* a disease of the vine, was made a baron by the King of Portugal for his services to wine. He drowned in 1862 when his boat capsized on the Douro, weighed down by the gold coins in his money belt. Forrester and Co. still exist and

(e) The opening of the Junction (Princes) Dock, 1829, the Trinity House yacht **Ariel** *entering the Junction Dock, drawn by the steam tug* **Kingston** *(9 x 11 in.); J. J. Forrester. (Town Docks Museum).*

market the Offley brand of port. Information kindly supplied by Roy Kaye, Chief Port Health Inspector).

FOX, John
Spent thirty years at sea as a marine engineer sailing all round the world. Entirely self-taught he started drawing at the age of 23 and later graduated to watercolours and oils. His canvases include nostalgic pictures of old sailing ships and vessels in the Hull docks; works from a studio in the garden of his home in Kirkella (*Select* (Beverley) February/March 1990, pp.8-10).

FRISTON, Frederick Edwin (fl.1880's)
Artist, carver and gilder at 31 Leonard Street, Hull, in 1885 and 3 Park Road in 1889. Listed as carver and gilder at 3 Old Market, Grimsby in 1877 and in 1882 is at 3 Market Place, Grimsby as artist and photographer, carver and gilder, living at Poplar Villa, Chantry Lane. A view of Grimsby harbour, signed and dated 1880 was sold as lot 118 by *Christies* (South Kensington), 25 April

1988, and an oil of the Grimsby fishing fleet as lot 118A. A simple profile of the smack *Harry Sinclair* was bought by the Welholme Gallery, Grimsby, in 1989. Several other members of the family are recorded in Hull; H. Friston, carver and gilder of Parker Street; S. Friston, engravers and artists colour shop in Savile Street (he showed a photograph of Martin Samuelson the shipbuilder at the 1870 exhibition and other photographic subjects; according to Galloway he engraved the books of Pierce Egan, the sporting writer), and a D. H. Friston exhibited gouache paintings at Hull in 1867 and 1870. A Samuel Friston, carver and gilder was at Toll Gavel, Beverley, in 1846 and also appears as an engraver of illustrations in Beetons Christmas Annual, notably the 1887 edition which featured A. Conan Doyle's *A Study in Scarlet*, in which Sherlock Holmes made his first appearance in print.

GAWTHORNE, H. G.
Lithographic poster, designed for the London and North

(f) A sketch of the position of some of the vessels at the late perilous fishery, laying in Baffin's Bay ($11^3/_4$ x $16^1/_2$ in.); E. Gibson, 1830. (Hull Trinity House).

Eastern Railway Co., entitled 'Hull, Britain's cheapest port' (TDM).

GIBSON, Edward (1787-1859)
Shipbuilder, amateur painter in watercolours and son of William Gibson founder of a Hull shipyard, he was Sheriff of Hull in 1814 and Mayor in 1834, 1835. Died at Eastgate House, Hornsea. Pen and wash of whaleship beset in Davis Straits, signed and dated 1830, in the Hull Trinity House. A newly discovered journal written by George Laing, surgeon of the whaleship *Zephyr* in 1830, contains a series of sketches of vessels beset in the ice which appear to be the foundation of the Gibson drawing (journal in possession of Mrs. J. Starke, New Zealand).

GILL, J. H. (fl.1859-1914)
This signature is clearly depicted on a painting of seals and ice floes with whalers beset, an oil painting in the Town Docks Museum. This is evidently the true ren-

dering of the name given as John M. Gell by Galloway in 1951. The catalogues of the 1897 and 1900 exhibition record him as J. M. Gill. A metal agent living at 46 Peel Street he is described in the 1889 directory as an artists colourman at 45 Chariot Street. At the Municipal Art Gallery in 1900 he exhibited two canvases of alpine scenes.

GOOCH, Edward Belton (1835-?)
Born at Selby gained his masters ticket at Sunderland in 1870. His last voyage was out of Hull as mate of the Bailey and Leetham vessel *Sultan* in 1899. Oil paintings of the S.S. *Ariosto*, dated 1897 and the *Eldorado*, 1898, are in the Town Docks Museum.

GOOD, Clements (1810-96)
Danish consul in Hull, he exhibited in 1889 and 1900. An oil of the Hull Citadel and watercolour entitled 'Falmouth for orders' with warships in harbour, dated 17 March 1897, are in the Town Docks Museum.

GOODIN, Walter (b.1907-1991)

Born and educated in Hull, a protege of Fred Elwell, R.A., he was trained at the Royal Academy Schools, where he was awarded the gold, silver and bronze medals. After the war he taught at Queen Margaret School, Bridlington, but since the 1950's, he continued to paint a wide variety of subjects. These include a number of views of the East Yorkshire coast including Filey, Bridlington, etc. Examples of his work are in private collections, at home and overseas, and in the hands of public companies including Reckitt and Colman. A retrospective exhibition was held at Sewerby Hall Museum and Art Gallery, 1-27 June 1991.

GRIFFITHS, Albert Edward (fl.1909-22)

A marine engineer he was living at 12 Victoria Avenue, Wellstead Street, 1909; was listed as a newsagent of 2 Victoria Parade, Hedon, around 1914, and foreman at 14 Cecil Street, 1921-2. Two paintings of the Hull trawler *Ribble* (H255) are in a private collection and it is probable that he served aboard this vessel.

* GRIFFIN, William (d. 1883)

HAKES, James Allen (1857-1927)

Painter and decorator his hobby was marine painting, mainly in oils, and he also made ship models. Works recorded include the Wilson Line vessel S.S. *Gozo* built 1868 at Earles Shipyard; also watercolours of S.S. *Dhoolier* and S.S. *Calcutta*. Lived and worked at 255 Anlaby Road and died at Sutton aged 70. See *Humber Light* (newsletter of the Hull branch of the World Ship Society) Vol.11, no.6, Nov-Dec 1976 pp.8-9. A steamship of the Wilson Line dated 1892 was lot 330 in Sotheby's *Marine Sale*, 3 June 1989.

HALL, H.

A gouache of the S.T. *Butterfly* (H393) built at Hull in 1898 for the British Steam Trawling Co., signed and dated 1909 (TDM).

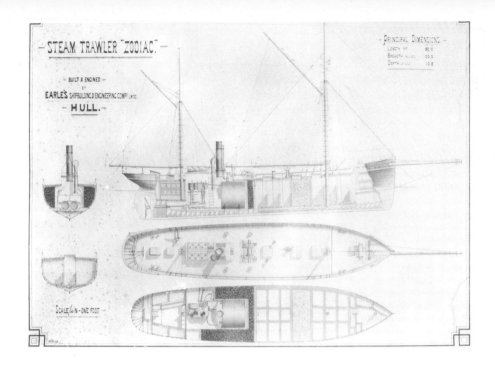

(h) The S.T. **Zodiac***; a hand-coloured general arrangement plan, signed R.P., 24 February 1882. (Town Docks Museum).*

HARE, Henry

Oil, small scale and delicately painted, signed and dated 1904. He was manager of the Kingston Enamelled Slate and Marble Co., brush, basket and umbrella maker and toy and fancy warehouse 32 and 33 Waterworks Street (h. West Park House) in 1881.

HARPER, John (1809-42)

Born near Blackburn, an architect and painter of topographical views and landscapes. Practised in York from 1835 where he became a close friend of William Etty. Considerable collection of his work in York City Art Gallery; a watercolour of the Old Harbour, Hull in the Ferens Art Gallery.

HARWOOD, A.

A pair of watercolours of the S.T. *Euripides* and a hospital ship signed and dated 1918 are in the Town Docks Museum. Three watercolours of steam trawlers with a Milford registration, signed and dated 1917 and 1918, appeared as lot 86 in Sotheby's *Marine Sale*, 5 June, 1985.

HAYWOOD, C. S.

Oil on board, Humber Keel under tow by paddle tug *Robin Hood* (TDM).

* HICK, Allanson (1898-1975)

HOLMES, George F. (1861-1940)

Engineer and founder member of the Humber Yawl Club (1883). Designer of canoe yawls he drew and painted on his many travels in Britain and on the continent. Frequently illustrated the cover of the Yawl Club Yearbook with his drawings and illustrated his descriptions of various cruises within its pages. He was a friend of Albert Strange and they often cruised together; there was clearly an interchange of ideas, Strange became a well known designer of small cruising yachts and Holmes work in this area was clearly an inspiration.

Strange himself was the head of the Scarborough Art School from 1882-1916 and would undoubtedly have helped Holmes in his artistic endeavours. Amongst the pupils whom Strange taught were the noted marine painters Frank Mason and Charles Pears, the latter the founder of the RSMA. Holmes produced a considerable number of small etchings some of them were intended as christmas greetings to his friends; examples in TDM. See *Humber Yawl Club Yearbook, 1940* for obituary notice, also John Leather *Albert Strange - yacht designer and artist, 1855-1917*, Edinburgh, 1990.

HOOPER, W.
Primitive painting in oils of first rate man of war firing broadside (TDM).

HORNER, Thomas B.
Lithograph of P.S. *Helen McGregor* (built 1843) by C. Hawkins after Horner who dedicates the print to Joseph Gee the vessel's owner (TDM).

HUSTWICK, Francis (?-1840)
In 1799 coach and heraldic painter to Robert Hustwick coachmaker; trio of loss of merchantman in FAG. Also portraits of Thomas Acland and genre pieces. 1799 commenced business as house, sign, ship and furniture painter at Savile Street near head of dock. Wilkinson and Hustwick, house, ship and sign and ornamental painters, 10 Posterngate (just commencing) 19 May 1827, *Hull Rockingham*. A Charles Hustwick also appears in the directories listed as a painter at 10 Albion Street in 1835.

HUTCHINSON, A.
Oil of the S.S. *Bhima*, built 1864 by Earles shipyard, Hull for the Bombay and Bengal Steamship Co. (TDM).

KOSKIE, Jack (b.1914)
Born in Hull he gained a scholarship to the Hull College of Art but at age 16 signed as a deckie learner on board a trawler. For a while he was a rivet heater in a local shipyard and the hard years of the 1930's forced him to drop out of his studies and take up a job in the printing industry. Emigrated to Australia in 1931 and served in the Merchant Navy and the army during the war. After ten years as a publisher's designer and illustrator he started teaching at Hobart Technical College in 1954 retiring in 1979 from a position as lecturer in print making at Deakin University. He has written articles on Australia's shipping heritage and contributed to the *Sydney Morning Herald*. His first book, *Ships that shaped Australia* published in 1981, in Australia, is entirely illustrated from his own oils. Celebrating the Bicentennial it starts with HMS *Endeavour* and concludes with *Australia II* winner of the America Cup.

LANE, C.A.
Oil of the sailing ship *Sea King*, lost 1867 (TDM).

* LUCOP, Charles (1828-1909)

* LUCOP, Thomas (fl. 1867-1907)

MALCOLM, A.
Watercolour, signed and dated 1882, of the Humber ferry P.S. *Manchester* (Manchester, Sheffield and Lincoln Railway Co.) off Victoria Pier (TDM).

MASON, W. L.
Oil on board, signed and dated 1902, of the Wilson Line vessel S.S. *Cito* (TDM).

MERRION, Jack
Lithographic poster for the Norther Eastern Railway 'Landing the catch at St. Andrews dock, Hull' (TDM).

MUMMERY, G. A.
Oil, signed and dated 20th September 1910, of tug *Goole No.10* towing *Clara* (TDM).

* NIXON, W. R. (fl. 1870-86)

NORTHWOOD, W.
Oil, signed an dated 1875; ship in full sail painted on

*(i) The steam yacht **Eira** (17 x 28 in.); W. Preston, 1889. (Town Docks Museum).*

cigar box lid (TDM).

ODLIN, George (b. 1947)

Oils and watercolours. Son, grandson and brother of mariners, an art teacher by profession and a keen yachtsman. Head of Art at Whitgift School, Grimsby where he is now deputy headmaster. Designer and producer of a decorative chart of the Humber. Main subjects are historic sailing vessels, yachts and trawlers. Commissioned by Faroes Sea Food to paint 1000 tons freezer trawler *Vestervon*, presented to the captain when vessel entered service. Has had an exhibition at the Grimsby Public Library. Sketches published in *Dalesman*, *Lincolnshire Life* and leading yachting magazines.

OVENDEN, F.W (Sometimes recorded as T.W.)

Exhibited once only at the Royal Academy, in 1836, 'item 281 Shore scene'. His address is given as 45 Carey Street, London, but an example of his work was in John Ward's studio at his death and a view of Bridlington quay (1841) appeared as lot 41 in Sotherbys, 'Marine Sale', 20 May 1992.

* PENNY, W. D. (1834-1924)

PRESTON, William

Oil of the S.S. *Eira* exploration ship of Benjamin Leigh Smith in the Arctic, built 1880, lost in 1881; S.S. *Seahorse* signed W. Preston, Hull, 1888 (TDM). An oil with the monogram W.P. is probably by the same artist. In private hands is a canvas signed W. Preston of the iron-hulled smack *Precursor* built at Hull by Cook, Welton and Gemmell in 1885. Roger Finch (*The Pierhead painters*, London, 1983) records canvases signed 'W. Preston, new Grimsby and Hull' and reproduces a painting of the *Albert* off Grimsby in 1861, a steamer built at Earles shipyard in 1856. No confirmation of a Grimsby connection can be discovered in the local trade directories.

*(j) The S.T. **Oakwold**, GY.948 (9 x 12 in.); G. Race, 1912. (Town Docks Museum).*

PRESTON, W. W. (and W. W. F.)
Oil on board of the paddle tugs *Antinichol*, *Hope*, *Powerful* and *Pilot* on the Humber (TDM).

RACE, George (1877-1952)
Born at Elm Avenue, New Clee, in 1877, he was one of four children. Married Martha Davey in 1896 and lived in a coastguard's cottage (Battery House) at Suggit's Lane which was washed away in a storm in 1915. Joined the army and was gassed and afterwards carried on with his trips down the coast visiting the various fishing ports. The bulk of his surviving work is of trawlers but also painted murals for the fish restaurant at Scartho and the 'tiger' mural and fairy cave at Wonderland. Painted trawlers of the Hull, Grimsby, Lowestoft and Yarmouth fleets and a large selection of his pictures are in the Grimsby and Lowestoft museums. An oil of the S.T. *Zenobia* signed G.R. 1892 and the S.T. *Oakwold* oil on board signed G. Race 1912 as well as a small picture in a lifebelt frame all in the Town Docks Museum. Race died in 1952 and is buried in Humberston cemetery. There are two lifebelt pictures (signed, dated 1921) of the Inverness registered steam drifters *Treasure Trove* and *County of Inverness* in the Fishertown Museum at Nairn; these must have been produced by the artist when the vessels visited Yarmouth or Lowestoft.

RAMSEY, T.
Oil, signed and dated 1889, of the S.T. *Mizpah* (TDM).

* REDMORE, E. K. (1859/60-1941)

* REDMORE, Henry (1820-87)

REMBRANDT VAN RIJN (1606-1669)
He is thought to have made two visits to England and according to the note books of George Vertue, in an entry written in 1713 'Rembrandt van Rhine was in England liv'd at Hull in Yorkshire about 15 or 18 months (reported by old Larroon who in his youth knew Rembrandt at York) where he painted several Gentlemen

and sea faring pictures. One of them is in the possession of Mr Dahl, a sea captain, with the Gentlemens name Rembrandts name and York and the year 1661-2'.

RENARD, Stephen (b. 1947)

Born at Huddersfield, and graduated at Liverpool University in the natural sciences. He spent three years at training college and, while head of Biology in a Liverpool school, developed a passionate interest in sailing. Abandoning teaching, Renard tried to make a living as a portrait artist, took lessons In ink drawing, and became a freelance illustrator of childrens comics. After purchasing a boat in 1981, he taught himself to sail and was painting ships as a hobby when he was advised to show his work to James Starkey of Beverley, art dealer. Since then he has concentrated on yachting subjects, following in the footsteps of Steven Dews. Recently the artist has been chosen by Rosenstiels, the fine art publishers, to produce four paintings suitable for making into prints. In addition he has been asked to work as the in-house artist for the Royal Thames Yacht Club and for his first commission produced a painting of the Spithead review, honouring the birthday of Queen Elizabeth the Queen Mother.

RHODES, F. O.

Watercolour, signed and dated 1879, of the topsail schooner *Melita* (TDM).

RIGG, Jack (b. 1927)

Born at Farsley, near Leeds he spent his early life in the textile industry but gained a love of the sea during service in the Royal Navy. It was the 1960's before he started painting seriously in his spare time and in 1978 Rigg gave up his regular job and began to paint professionally. His work has concentrated more on the east coast and the Humber estuary in recent years and he never copies from other illustrations or photographs, each scene is derived from the sketches made on a particular date in a particular place. Rigg is regularly

(k) St. Andrew's Dock extension (17 x 30 in.); F. S. Smith, 1895. (Town Docks Museum).

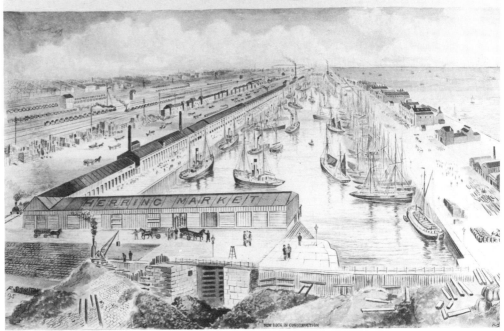

commissioned by shipowners and maritime organisations, and for three of the last four years his work has been selected to illustrate the RNMDSF Christmas Card. Pictures have been exhibited all over the north of England and in London and his paintings or reproductions of them have found their way to Buckingham Palace and the White House.

* RODMELL, H. H. (1896-1984)

SCOTT, J.
Oil, signed and dated 1861, of the *Emma Ash* (TDM).

SEARLE, Peter
An Australian, born at Narrabundah, New South Wales, painter and model maker. As a young man sailed round the Pacific in the bark *Stettin*; served in the Royal Australian navy until transferred to the RN in 1939 and saw war service in submarines and aboard aircraft carriers in the Russian convoys. Stayed in England after leaving the navy in 1947 and joined the Humber Conservancy to work in pilot cutters. See *Hull Daily Mail*, 25 March 1977 which illustrates his picture of the steam pilot cutter *Wm. Fenton* which he painted for the Oberon Hotel in Queen Street; two other marines of clippers hang in the Victoria Dock Tavern.

* SETTLE, W. F. (1821-1897)

SEWARD, P. C.
Oil, signed and dated 1881, of the Humber ferry P.S. *Sheffield* (Manchester, Sheffield and Lincoln Railway Co.) (TDM).

SMITH, F. S. (1860-1925)
Topographical artist, some of his drawing depict the Hull docks e.g. a 'bird's eye view' of the fish dock, signed and dated 1895; also a drawing of the T.S. *Southampton* with HMS *Endymion*, a guard ship, signed and dated 1888 (TDM). See C. Aldridge *Images of*

Victorian Hull, Hull, 1989 and C. Ketchell *F. S. Smith's drawings of Hull*, Hull, 1990.

SNOW, W. H.
Oils of the S.S. *Zebra* and S.S. *Falcon*, formerly belonging to Brownlow Lumsden depicted in the livery of the Wilson Line to whom they were sold in 1880 and 1878 respectively. Also a lithograph of 'Scarborough from the sea' after H. B. Carter (TDM).

SOLOMON, R.
Watercolour, signed and dated 1871 of S.S. *Sprite* (TDM).

* SOMERSCALES, T. J. (1842-1927)

SPENCE, Samuel John
Marine and landscape painter, died in his 29th year, 5 July 1879 (*Hull Packet*, 11 July 1879).

SPENCER, James
Shipbuilder; a draft signed and dated 1805 of the brig *Faith* (TDM).

STEWART, A. J.
Oil, signed and dated 1881, of vessels of the box fleet (TDM) and another depicting six Hull smacks, including the Clio, Stella, Atlas, Milo and Lizzie.

STUBBS, Ralph (1774-1845)
Stubbs Snr. who apparently lived on the continent for some twenty years and served as an interpreter with Wellington's army settled at Bridlington Quay in 1821. A certain G. Stubbs had a Reading Room, Circulating Library, Artists and English Stationery Repository in Boulogne, established in 1819 at 4 Rue de l'Ecu; he was also a dealer in 'Genuine teas, Burton ales, and Brown Stout', A. Stubbs had a warehouse for 'Ancient furniture and Wood Carvings' at 37 Rue de Bras. Ralph taught

(m) A squall coming off Folkestone (20 x 30 in.); R. Stubbs, 1854. (Messrs. Sotheby).

drawing and French and advertised himself as a 'restorer of old pictures' and in July 1823 married Miss Mary Baron of Catwick describing himself as 'artist and proprietor of the Reading Rooms, Bridlington'. His output consisted mainly of Yorkshire landscapes and it is not always easy to disentangle his work from that of his son of the same name. Latterly he may have resided in Hull for the announcement of his death which occured on the 4th January, 1845, aged 71, in the Hull press, describes him as 'of this place artist much and deservedly respected'. R. Stubbs, father and son, were paid for unspecified work at Burton Constable Hall in 1844.

STUBBS, Ralph (1823-79)

Though he produced a number of pleasing marine studies, the younger Stubbs painted mainly views of the Yorkshire countryside in the northern part of the country, such as Fylingdales and Rievaulx Abbey and he died at Levisham near Whitby in 1879. There is no evidence that he ever resided in Hull on any regular basis though an entry in the 1848 trade directory recording a Reuben Stubbs painter living at 11 George Street may be an error and in fact refer to Ralph. He is said to have been persuaded by R. Collinson a collector of his works at Scarborough to exhibit for the first time at the Royal Academy in 1872 and he followed this in 1873 with a picture entitled 'The Beggars Bridge' taken from a view at Egton near Whitby. A Samuel Stubbs, painter is also recorded as working in Hull in the early nineteenth century and James Stubbs was responsible for two views of the Market Place, lithographed in 1848 and 1850.

THOMPSON, Adrian (b. 1960)

Fitters mate with British Rail at York; after leaving school did not try any drawing until Summer of 1985 and at christmas that year was given an instruction book on watercolour painting. He works from photographs of vessels long vanished or of photographs of current vessels which he or his brother Mike Thompson have taken. First exhibited his work at the Town Docks Museum and in 1986 his watercolour of the *Arctic*

Corsair was issued as a print (*The Star*, 27 November 1986). Has exhibited at the Ferens Winter Exhibition; the *Junella* was used as cover design of Mike Thompson's *Hull and Grimsby Stern Trawling Fleet, 1961-88* (1988).

THOMPSON, E.

Watercolour, signed and dated 1892, of the S.S. *Thomas Wilson*.

THOMPSON, Tim (b. 1951)

Born in Hull he spent much of his childhood on Herm in the Channel Islands where he taught himself to paint. After a career in horticulture was cut short in 1979 by an accident he decided to make art a full-time career. Has had several exhibitions and provided the illustrations for Ranulf Rayner, *The Paintings of the America Cup, 1851-1897*, (1986). This series of twenty-six oil paintings took two years to complete and was exhibited at Perth in the run up to the Americas Cup series in Australia (*Daily Telegraph* 13 October, 1986). The artist now lives in Saltash in Devon, in a house overlooking the Tamar river.

* TINDALL, Benjamin (fl. 1840-89)

TUTILL, G. W.

His wife Emma died in London aged 25; he is described late of Hull (*H.A.* 3 December 1841). Oil on panel signed and dated 1864 of the first steamer in the Humber; this is apparently a fiftieth anniversary painting of the P.S. *Caledonia* which entered service in 1814 (TDM).

USHER, J. W.

Oil of the Bailey and Leetham steamer *Kotka* built 1884 (TDM).

* VERITY, Colin (b. 1924)
* WARD, John (1798-1849)

WELBURN, Bill
Oil, signed and dated 1967, of the stern trawler *Junella* (TDM).

* WHELDALE, James and George (fl. 1839-55)
* WHELDON, James (1832-93)

* WIDDAS, R. D. (1826-85)

WILKINSON, Jeffrey
Watercolour of the trawler *St. Giles* (H220) signed and dated 22 February 1968 (TDM).
WILLIAMSON, John

* WILLOUGHBY, Robert (1768-1843); and other members of the Willoughby family.

* WILSON, S. H. (fl. 1855-80)

WILSON, Will
Watercolour of the S.T. *Lord Heneage* (H.27) signed and dated, 'Will. Wilson 1909'; the vessel was launched that year (TDM).

WISEMAN, George
Watercolour of trawler *Dayspring* (H.183) signed and dated 1969; also the Grimsby trawler *Vanessa*, dated 1955, and the *St. Keverne*, undated (TDM).

WOOLSTON, Geoff
Graduate of Manchester Art College and professional illustrator before joining staff of the Hull Daily Mail. His print of the 'Horsewash, Hull, 1949' was sold in a limited edition of 850 as part of the newspapers centenary celebrations (*The Star*, 13 Nov., 1986).

YATES, Norman (b. 1892-d. 1974)
Born at Newcastle he first went to sea aged 14 aboard the bark *Kildalton* and was a seasoned Cape Horner. Later an officer with the Wilson Line he was a Lieutenant RNR in the Great War in command of an anti-submarine vessel. Joined the Humber Pilot Service in 1922 and was active in the 1939-45 war as a Lieutenant Commander in the Humber Examination Service, Naval Control and from D-Day was active as a Southampton and Channel pilot with Combined Operations. He retired from the pilot service in 1948. He held an extra masters square-rigged certificate and it was the big sailing vessels of his youth which retained an abiding fascination for him when he took up painting as a hobby. These were mainly watercolours of the ships he had sailed in or had encountered in his voyaging. A display of his work was shown at the Hull Central Library in 1973 and he contributed to the Ferens Winter Exhibition the previous year. Watercolours, documents, personalia and a copy of his memoirs are all in the Town Docks Museum.

ART EXHIBITIONS IN HULL 1827-1900

The Hull and East Riding Institution for the Promotion of the Fine Arts, Hull, 1827
Catalogue of exhibition which opened 23 July 1827, the foundation year of the Institution.

Hull and East Riding Institution for the Promotion of the Fine Arts, Hull, 1829.
Catalogue of second and last exhibition of the Institution.

Catalogue of the Exhibition of the Fine Arts, Kingston Square, Hull, 1835.

Catalogue of the Grand Polytechnic Exhibition of Objects Illustrative of the Fine Arts, Natural History, Philosophy, Machinery, Antiquities, etc. at the Mechanics Institution, George Street, Hull, 1845.

Hull School of Art; Local Catalogue of the Ancient and Modern Paintings etc. in the Art Exhibition, Art Gallery, Kingston Square, February, 1862, Hull, 1862.

Hull School of Art, Second Exhibition, Catalogue of Modern Paintings, Art Workmanship etc., Art Gallery, Kingston Square, February 1864, Hull 1864.

Official Catalogue of the Working Mens Art, Industrial and General Exhibition, Opened 20 June 1870, Hull, 1870.

Hull and District Art and Industrial Exhibition under the auspices of the Hull and District Band of Hope League, Artillery Barracks, Hull, opened May 7, 1878, Hull, 1878.

Hull Literary and Philosophical Society; Special Loan Art Collection, Hull, 1878.

Hull Temperance Club, 8 Albion Street, Exhibition of the Works of Local Artists, April 1881, Hull, 1881.

Catalogue of the Marine Exhibition held in the Artillery Barracks, Hull, in aid of the National Lifeboat Institution and the Kingston Model Yacht Club, March 5th-17th, Hull, 1883.

Hull, Yorkshire and Lincolnshire Fine Arts and Historical Exhibition in aid of the Hull General Infirmary at the Public Rooms, Hull, 1883.

Descriptive Catalogue of a collection of Art Treasures and Antique Curiosities, selected from the museum at Winterton Hall, the property of and exhibited by M. W. Clarke, Esq. at the Infirmary Centenary Art Exhibition in the Music Hall, Jarratt Street, Hull, 1883.

Hull Fine Art Gallery, Summer Exhibition, 1889, Royal Institution, Albion Street, Hull, 1889.

Hull Fine Art Gallery, Autumn Exhibition 1890, Royal Institution, Albion Street, Hull, 1890.

Industrial Arts and Manufacturers Exhibition, Artillery Barracks, 7 October - 8 November 1893, Hull, 1893.

Society of Arts Exhibition, May 1896.
Held at the Royal Institution, Albion Street.

Municipal Art Gallery, Catalogue of First Exhibition of Modern Works of Art, May 1900.
(The Royal Institution, Albion Street; from 1900 this was the home of the Municipal Museum and Art Gallery, the latter subsequently moved to the Mortimer Galleries and finally the Ferens Art Gallery).
Municipal Art Gallery, Catalogue of the First Autumn Exhibition of Modern Works of Art, October, 1900. (Albion Street).

IMPORTANT SALES OF WORKS OF ART IN HULL (1843-87)

Catalogue of the Gallery of Pictures known as the Wharton collection consisting of about 150 specimens of the most celebrated masters of the Italian, Flemish and Dutch schools which will be submitted to Public competition and unreserved sale by Mr. Stamp, on Wednesday and Thursday the 14 and 15 June 1843 in the salon of the Mechanics Institute, George Street, Hull.

A Catalogue of the remaining articles of genteel household furniture, cottage piano forte, library of books, collection of oil paintings, cellar of wine, Britzka carriage, pony phaeton, two sets of harness and other effects. Auctioned by Charles Johnson at the home of the late George Cammell, 24 February, 1858.

The Earle Collection; Catalogue of the private gallery of oil paintings the property of an eminent connoisseur (G. F. Earle).
Auctioned by Charles Johnson in the large sale room, George Hotel, Hull, 26 April, 1877.

The Sykes Collection; Catalogue of the private gallery of oil paintings.
(Property of James Sykes. Sold by auction 12 December by Charles Johnson at the large room, George Hotel), Hull, 1877.

A Catalogue of the celebrated Collection of Pictures the property of William Hodson, deceased.
(Sold by N. Easton and Son at the Fine Art Gallery, Imperial Chambers, Bowlalley Lane, 9 August), Hull, 1878.

Catalogue of the valuable collection of oil paintings, side board of silver plate, etc. of the late Anthony Bannister Esq.

Auctioned by Charles Johnson at Messrs. N. Easton and Sons, Fine Art Gallery, Bowlalley Lane, 5 September, 1878.

A Catalogue of the Collection of High Class Modern Oil Paintings the property of W. Beckett Esq., 65 Peel Street.
(Sold by N. Easton and Son at the Fine Art Gallery, Imperial Chambers, Bowlalley Lane, 22 December) Hull, 1879.

The Collection of Oil Paintings, Watercolour Drawings, Bronzes, Illustrated books, etc. The property of G. H. Earle Esq., Linnaeus House.
(Sold by Charles Johnson, in the large room, George Hotel, 13 May) Hull, 1880.

Sale by private treaty only of thirty two ancient and modern valuable Oil Paintings being the fourth and remaining portion of the collection of the late John Yourell Esq. Ballymacarney, Co. Dublin.
(Sold by Joshua Tewson, Sale Rooms, 37 Lowgate, 9 June) Hull, 1880.

A Catalogue of the well-known collection of rare porcelain and pottery, the antique silver, ancient and modern jewellery, oil paintings and watercolours, coins, illustrated books, carved oak furniture; by order of the executors of M. W. Clarke Esq. deceased of Winterton Hall and Hull; which N. Easton and Son will sell by auction, 6 and 7 July, Hull, 1887.

SOURCES

Parish registers *passim*, located at the County Record Office, Beverley the *Hull Advertiser, Hull Packet* and *Eastern Morning News* from the originals and microfilms held at the Local Studies Library, Albion Street, Hull

A great many details were ascertained through extensive correspondence, all of which is filed in the Town Docks Museum.

(Antique Collectors Club), *Works Exhibited at the Royal Society of British Artists 1824-93 and at the New English Art Club 1888-1917*, London, 1975.

E. H. H. Archibald, *Dictionary of Sea Painters*, Woodbridge, 1980.

M. V. and D. Brewington, *Marine Paintings and Drawings in the Peabody Museum*, Salem, Massachusetts, 1968.

Colin P. Bullamore, *Scarborough and Whitby Watercolours*, Whitby, 1976.

Rotha Mary Clay, *Julius Caesar Ibbetson, 1759-1817*, London, 1948.

J. N. Crosse, *An Account of the Rise and Progress of the Subscription Library at Kingston upon Hull*, Hull, 1810.

Malcolm Elwin, *The Autobiography and Journals of Benjamin Robert Haydon, 1786-1846*, London, 1950 (report of 1883 edition).

Vincent Galloway, *Early Marine Paintings and Hull Art Directory*, Ferens Art Gallery, Hull, 1951 (Festival of Britain Exhibition).

Algernon Graves, *The British Institution 1806-67 - a complete dictionary of Contributors and their work from the foundation of the Institution*, London, 1875.

Algernon Graves, *The Royal Academy of Arts - A complete dictionary of Exhibitions 1769-1904*, 4 vols., London, 1908.

Alex A. Hurst, *Thomas Somerscales - Marine Artist*, Brighton, 1987.

Jacob Larwood and John Camden Hotten, *The History of Signboards*, London, 1884.

J. T. Smith, *Nollekens and his times*, London, 1895.

Anthony Steel, *History of St. Mary's Church, Lockington*, Lockington, 1975.

John Wilton-Ely, editor, *A Tercentenary tribute to William Kent*, Ferens Art Gallery, Hull, 1985.

NOTES

Introduction

1. Ed. James Greig *The Farington Diary*, London, 1923, vol.3, pp48-9, entries for 1805.
2. Rotha Mary Clay, *Julius Caesar Ibbetson 1759-1817*, London, 1948.
3. Pieter van der Merwe, *Clarkson Stanfield 1793-1867*, Tyne and Wear County Council Museums, 1979; catalogue of an exhibition held at Sunderland the artists's birthplace. Stanfield, George Chambers and de Loutherbourg all worked as scene painters during their careers.
4. See historical essay which follows the introduction.
5. Sidney C. Hutchison, *The History of the Royal Academy, 1768-1986*, London, 1986.
   One of the functions of the RA was to provide support to indigent artists and their families. Charles Brooking who is now acknowledged as one of the masters of the British school of marine painting died at the early age of thirty six and left his family in difficult circumstances. In 1769 £11 was paid out of the Royal Academy's funds to enable one of his sons to be apprenticed to a peruke maker. This donation was very probably given under the particular recommendation of Dominic Serres, a founder member and marine painter to the King, who knew Brooking well and was much influenced by him as an artist.
6. *ibid*.
7. Trevor Fawcett, *The Rise of English Provincial Art*, Oxford, 1974.
8. From 1895 the School of Art was attached to the Municipal Technical School but split off again and was established in new premises on the Anlaby Road in 1905. Renamed the Hull College of Arts and Crafts it embraced three schools; architecture; industrial design and crafts; drawing and painting.
9. *The Hull and East Riding Institution for the Promotion of the Fine Arts*, Hull, 1827; catalogue of first exhibition.
10. *The Second Exhibition of the Hull and East Riding Institution for the Promotion of the Fine Arts*, Hull, 1829.
11. The Hull Subscription Library, founded 1775, was the precursor of both the Literary and Philosophical Society and the local Mechanics Institute and had attempted to promote adult education through both literary and scientific activities. The Lit. and Phil. tended to be restricted in its membership to the merchants and professional men of the city, as had the Subscription Library, but it also supported regular series of lectures open to a wider public. The Mechanics Institute had a much broader constituency appealing to artists, artisans and ordinary citizens seeking to broaden their horizons.
    As early as 1804 Dr. Alderson had encouraged the Hull Subscription Library to vote £50 annually for a lecture course on scientific and commercial subjects and in 1805 George Birkbeck, who was the founding father of the Mechanic's Institute movement, gave two courses in natural and mechanical philosophy (See C. Frost, *An address delivered to the Literary and Philosophical Society at Kingston upon Hull, Friday, Nov. 30, 1830*, Hull, 1831, pp.60-1).
12. T. W. Wallis *The autobiography of Thomas Wilkinson Wallis, sculptor in wood*, Louth, 1899; born in Hull 1821, apprenticed to Thomas Ward, carver and gilder, exhibited at the Great Exhibition in 1851 and was latterly borough surveyor of Louth where he died in 1903.
13. *ibid* p.48. T. W. Wallis's cousin Edward Wallis, MRCS, lecturer at the Hull School of Medicine gave a series of lectures at the Institute 'On human and comparative anatomy and physiology'.
14. This is described in a booklet entitled: *An historical sketch with a descriptive outline of the grand moving peristrephic panorama of the siege of Hull in 1643*, Hull 1829. Painted by the local artists over a period of two years it was displayed in Kirkwood's Olympic circus.
15. The Mechanics Institute was certainly thriving in 1828 with 794 members, an income of over £354 and 2230 volumes in its library.

16. C. H. Ward-Jackson, *Reuben Chappell 1870-1940*, 1970; catalogue of an exhibition held at Bristol and the National Maritime Museum, Greenwich.

Origins and Progress

17. John Thomas Smith, *Nollekens and his times*, London, 1828, pp.18-19.
18. Rotha Mary Clay, *Julius Caesar Ibbetson 1759-1817*, London, 1948.
19. Benjamin Gale (1741-1832) artist and drawing master, executed many of the pictures engraved for John Tickell's *History of Hull 1798*, and also portraits of Andrew Marvell, the Rev. Thomas Browne (poet and editor of *Hull Advertiser)* as well as a self-portrait. Perhaps the son of Matthew Gale, a Hull stonemason he died at Bridlington Quay, aged 91.
20. Ed. Judy Egerton, *George Stubbs 1724-1806*, London, 1984/5; catalogue of exhibition held at the Tate Gallery.
21. A. G. Credland, 'Wallis of Hull', *Journal of the Arms and Armour Society*, vol.9, no.4, December 1978, pp.133-85; Ralph Edwards, 'J. R. Smith and his pupils', *Connoisseur*, 1934, pp.96-101.
22. Ed. J. Wilton-Ely, *A Tercentenary tribute to William Kent, 1685-1784*, Hull, 1985. The diary of George Vertue has the following: 'When young unexpectedly demonstrated his youthful inclininations to drawing. Being apprentice of a coach painter and house painter (in Hull) - from him he came to London with out leave or finishing his apprenticeship'.
23. A fine portait which hangs in the Town Docks Museum, Hull; the Sykes portrait is in the Hull Guildhall and the full length of King George is still in the Trinity House.
24. Robert Thew (1758-1802); had the patronage of the Duke of Leeds and was appointed to his post as engraver to the Prince of Wales at the recommendation of Charles Fox, the Duchess of Devonshire and Lady Duncannon. See *Gen tleman's Magazine*, 1802, vol.72, pt.2, pp.971-2 and 1803 vol.73 pt.1, p.475.
25. But see note 29.
26. Hangs in the Town Docks Museum, Hull.
27. Anon. (J. N. Crosse) *An account of the rise and progress of the Subscription Library at Kingston upon Hull, established 6 December 1775*, Hull, 1810. Crosse was a Baltic merchant and committee member of the Hull and East Riding Institution for the Promotion of the Fine Arts.
28. James Rush, *The Ingenious Beilbys*, London, 1973; and J. Rush *A Beilby Odyssey*, Olney, 1987.
29. The pair of oval canvases in the Hull Trinity House depicting the trading vessel *Mayflower* are possibly early works by Whitcombe but this is a suggestion based on stylistic grands, there is no documentary support for this.
30. John Watkins *Life and career of George Chambers*, London, 1841; went to sea at age of sixteen in the Humber Keel *Experiment* belonging to his uncle; decorated the 'Waterman's Arms', Wapping, with scenes of Whitby and was employed by Hornor, a Hull man, in painting the great *Diorama* at the Colosseum. Later he received the patronage of Admiral Capell and King William 4 but died at the early age of thirty-seven.
31. *Hull Advertiser*, 21 June, 1800.
32. A. G. Credland, 'Moby Dick, Hull and East Yorkshire', *Great Circle (Journal of the Australian Association for Maritime History)* vol.11, no.1, 1989, pp.44-54.
33. *Hull Advertiser*, 18 March, 1836.
34. *Hull Rockingham*, 11 November, 1837.
35. Harold S. Sniffen, *Antonio Jacobsen - the checklist*, New York, 1984.
36. Ernest Butler, *Reuben Chappell 1870-1944, The Goole Marine Artist*, catalogue of a loan exhibition held at Goole, Doncaster, Scunthorpe, 1972-3.

Thomas Fletcher

37. Town Docks Museum. Sadler was known as 'But' Sadler for his habit of prefacing his sentences with that word. He was onc of Hull's most successful whaling captains and the 44 Right whales caught in 1804 stands as an all-time record for the Arctic fishery. For a brief biography and portrait see *Hull and East Riding Portfolio*, vol.2, 1885, pp.161-4.
38. Very similar illustrations but in a different arrangement appear in the trade card of John Browne, compass maker and ship chandler of Wapping Old Stairs, London. See H. R. Calvert, *Scientific Trade Cards*, London, 1971. Another trade card of similar composition was engraved by Hilbert for Joseph Hall, a local cabinet maker; see C. Hutchinson *Furniture*

made in Yorkshire 1750-1900, Leeds, 1974.

39. See Ivan and Elizabeth Hall, *A new picture of Georgian Hull*, York, 1978-9, p.8.
40. M. E. Ingram, *Our Lady of Hull*, 1948, pp.94-5.
41. A quote from Farington's diary; see R. M. Clay *op.cit*, p.5.
42. Tate Wilkinson, *Wanderings of a patentee*, 1795, p.213.
43. Anyone consulting the parish registers of Holy Trinity Church will be familiar with their names. A copy of a 1791 entry in the registers made as a result of an enquiry is signed and dated 'Examined the 8th day of January 1808 by me, Rouncival Fletcher, licensed clerk and register (sic)'.
44. M. C. Peck '*A sketch of the history of the Minerva Chapter, no.250, Hull* ', Hull, 1887, pp.5-6. Initially meetings were held at the Mason's Arms, Chapel Lane but a lodge was opened in Dagger Lane in 1802. These premises including the masonic temple in its original form are used to this day.
45. Rouncival and his wife had at least five children between 1799 and 1808, Eleanor, William, Rouncival, Winefred (sic), and Thomas. A manuscript in the library of the Society of Genealogists records the baptisms at the Roman Catholic Chapel, formerly in North Street later in Jarratt Street. All of these children were also baptised at Holy Trinity Church. The spelling of Rouncival varies, sometimes with an *e* instead of an *i* and with an *s* instead of the *c*. The manuscript spells his wifes name Winefred, the parish registers of Holy Trinity have the form Winnifred.
46. *Hull Advertiser*, 2 January 1824; he was buried on that day, a Friday.
47. The registers of Holy Trinity Church record his baptism 31 July 1804.
48. *Hull Advertiser*, 23 January, 1824.

Robert Willoughby

49. From an address 'near the new Gaol', he was advertising for two journeymen to be engaged by the year; *Hull Advertiser*, 2 March, 1799.
50. Dated canvases include, an unnamed whaler 1807, the *Elizabeth and Leviathan*, 1811 and the *Gilder*, 1813; the latter is inscribed '1813 R. Willoughby' on the dead whale being towed across the foreground.
51. Illustrated in J. Simmonds *Kingstoniana* Hull,

1839, facing page 12. Described as being in the possession of W. Wilkinson Esq., Hull. This and the companion piece (see below) are now in the Ferens Art Gallery, Hull.
52. This hangs in Wilberforce House, Hull.
53. Eliza neice of Dr. John Alderson was the wife of Henry Perronet Briggs while Amelia, another neice, daughter of James Alderson of Norwich and Amelia Briggs, was the wife of the artist, John Opie (1761-1807).
54. *Hull Advertiser*, 24 January 1807; R. Willoughby, house, ship and sign painter, thanks public for their patronage at his High Street (New George Yard) premises and announces his move to Savile Street. The by-line gives his home address as Castle Row.
55. *Hull Packet* 20 October 1812.
56. *Hull Packet* 10 November 1812; *Hull Rockingham*, 7 November 1812.
57. John, 3 June 1793; Margaret, 1794; Elizabeth, 1795; Robert, 1797 and Ralph, 1802.
58. *Hull Advertiser*, 3 November 1826. It is possible that the Willoughby's originated in Boston or maybe this was Elizabeth Willoughby's home town.
59. 2 March, 1797.
60. *Hull Rockingham*, 4 January 1823. The reference to Julius Caesar Ibbetson (1759-1817) links us back to John Fletcher to whom Ibbetson was apprenticed 1772-7.
61. *Hull Advertiser*, 16 November, 1827.It is probably no coincidence that this was the year in which the Hull and East Riding Institution for the Promotion of Fine Arts was Established.
62. *Hull Advertiser*, 22 July, 1831; a brother Thomas had died aged twenty-two, nine years earlier (*Hull Rockingham*, 3 August 1822).
63. See catalogue of the exhibition *op.cit*, item 54; the *Hull Advertiser* 2 November, 1827, notes that it was sold.
64. *ibid*, item 192.
65. A portrait of a woman in hunting clothes seated in a chair, dated 1817 passed through the Simon Carter gallery in 1987 and another female portrait of an elderly woman with lace cap, dated Dec. 1839, painted on panel was in local hands in 1989. There is also an unidentified picture of a merchant captain holding a sextant, with a sailing ship in the background, at the National Maritime Museum, Greenwich.
66. *Hull Advertiser*, 2 October 1858. If he is the

son of Elizabeth and Robert (see note 58) the age cannot be correct! Earlier that year an infant son Walter had died aged three (*Hull Advertiser*, 26 June 1858) and in 1878 John Henry 'youngest son of the late John Willoughby, painter of the town died at Portsmouth (*Hull and Eastern Counties Herald*, 10 January 1878).

William Barton

67. Originally offered in derelict condition at *Christies* sale, 22 November 1985, but after restoration was purchased from the Fulda Gallery for the Ferens Art Gallery.

68. Christies, *Maritime Sale*, London, 22-3 September 1988, lot 15.

69. Illustrated in Tindall Wildridge *Old and New Hull*, Hull, 1889, pp.159-60 entitled the 'Mouth of the river Hull' and the 'Old South End'; both are dated 1809. Then in the hands of Henry Livingston but Vincent Galloway (1951) recorded that they belonged to the Hull Literary and Philosophical Society at the beginning of the 1939-45 war and were destroyed in their Albion Street premises during the blitz. Clearly they survived the air-raids or were withdrawn from the Royal Institution prior to hostilities. The two panels reappeared in London in 1984 and were purchased for the Ferens Art Gallery (see also N. R. Omell, *Marine Paintings of the 18th, 19th and 20th Century*, London, 1984, lots 5 and 6 when they were erroneously ascribed to John Ward).

70. Ralph Hyde, *Panoramania*, London 1908; catalogue of an exhibition at the Barbican Art Gallery, 1988-9.

71. Stephen Oetterman *Das Panorama die geschichte eines Massenmedium*, Frankfurt am Main, 1980. I am indebted to the author for supplying the details of Barton's activities in Europe.

72. *Hull Advertiser*, 24 November 1798.

73. *Hull Advertiser*, 11 October 1800.

74. *Hull Advertiser*, 23 September 1836; the showing on 4 November that year was a benefit in aid of the families of the crew of the whaler *William Torr* lost in the Davis Strait fishery.

75. *An historical sketch of the grand moving peristrephic panorama, op cit.*

76. Richard D. Altick, *The Shows of London*, London 1978, p.195 etc. Before starting his

great Diorama project at the Colosseum Thomas Hornor had painted panoramic views of gentlemen's estates; from 1814-20 he worked in the Neath valley in South Wales. See Dr. R. G. Howell, *Under Sail - Swansea cutters, tall ships and seascape, 1830-80* Swansea, 1987, catalogue of an exhibition at the Glyn Vivian Art Gallery.

Thomas Meggitt, Thomas Binks

77. *Hull Packet, 7 July* 1800; *Hull Advertiser*, 5 July 1800; in the same issue William Benison declines his business in favour of T. Meggitt.

78. *Hull Packet*, 24 March, 1812.

79. It is signed *Meggitt jun. del.* The younger Meggitt was baptised on the 12 April 1803 at Holy Trinity Church having been born on the 2 February of the same year. His mother Jane Meggitt, nee Smith, died in 1813 at the age of thirty-two years. In 1839 Meggitt undertook a variety of tasks at Burton Constable Hall, these included the supply of 'a magic lantern painting' a 'screen painting on wire gauge', japanning a cigar case as well as cleaning pictures, repairing and gilding picture frames, glazing and varnishing woodwork. The firm also cleaned the figures and vases in the garden. (See vouchers in the County Record Office, Beverley).

80. After 1826 'house and ship painter' is deleted from the entries in the trade directories (except in 1848) in favour of 'painter and japanner' or 'Painters, japanners, gilders and decorators (1842-4; 1857-9).

81. See also *Hull and Eastern Counties Herald*, 24 November 1842; this wrongly gives the age as thirty-seven years. His wife Mary Ann died aged thirty-seven, at Kings Lynn, on 11 May 1844.

82. He bequeathed all of his drawing books 'and things in my museum' to his grandson Thomas Allen Meggitt, on condition he pursued the business of painter; evidently he declined the offer. The deceased had a brother, Samuel Meggitt, master mariner, who was living at Manor House Street in 1851.

83. Catalogue of the 1827 exhibition *op.cit*, item 250.

84. Photo-copy in the museum archive.

85. Grimston Garth was built 1781-6 by John Carr of York and is a charming example of Georgian gothic.

86. *Working Mens art, industrial and general exhibition*, Hull, 1870, item 491, lent by F. Jackson and ascribed simply to Binks. The *Kingston* was the first locally built steamship to enter regular service on the Humber, starting in 1821.

87. Both the *Kingston* and *Prince Frederick* were run by Weddle and Brownlow for the Hull Steam Packet Co.; the *Calder* belonged to the Aire and Calder Navigation Co. which had developed the port of Goole.

88. Catalogue of the *Marine Exhibition*, Hull, 1883; item 236d 'Whaling ships beset in the ice in Davis Strait', 1835, by Binks.

89. *Eastern Counties Herald*, 11 November, 1852.

90. A John Green appears in the 1839 directory as a painter in Cooperage Yard.

91. There is an advertisement in Melville's Hull directory of 1855 for 'Sculcoates oil boiling, refining and varnish works, Oxford Street. Oil sent from all parts of the town free of expense on orders being left at the office, 196 High Street, Wm. Binks and Son'. In 1846 Henry the brother of William Binks Snr. left the business and set up on his own account; unattributed note dated 30 April 1840 in the museum archives.

92. *Eastern Counties Herald*, 24 November, 1842; he died in his forty-ninth year.

93. Anthony Steel, *History of St. Mary's Church, Lockington*, 1975.

94. Ivan and Elizabeth Hall, *A new picture of Georgian Hull*, Hull, 1978-9, pp.105 and 109.

95. Information from a descendant of the Binks family and various sources including parish registers and newspapers.

William and Reuben Griffin

96. Who married Elizabeth Gibson at Holy Trinity Church, 18 October, 1781.

97. Ferens Art Gallery.

98. A printed label on the back incorrectly renders the artist's name as Griffiths.

99. Christies *Fine Victorian Pictures*, 7 October 1983, lot 155. It was shown at the Ferens Art Gallery, Festival of Britain exhibition in 1951.

100. In the hands of N. R. Omell in 1984. The *Herculaneum* though registered in Liverpool, sailed from Hull to Calcutta in that year. In 1842 it sailed to the same destination from Liverpool but then disappears from Lloyds register.

101. Item 207.

102. Christies, 5 October, 1984, lot 1.

103. Town Docks Museum, Hull.

104. *ibid.*

105. *ibid.*

106. Capt. D. Thompson, *A History of the Hull Trinity House School*, Hull, 1988.

107. Registers of Holy Trinity Church, Hull.

John Ward

108. Apparently he was born in Hull but no record of his baptism has been found. John's mother Sarah died aged fifty on the 19th April, 1814, but Abraham Ward was married a second time the following year to another Sarah who died in March 1824 at the age of forty nine. These events are recorded in the parish registers of Holy Trinity Church and in an associated volume in which are copied the inscriptions from headstones and memorials now destroyed. Abraham Ward himself died in 1836 at the age of seventy five.

109. *Eastern Morning News*, February, 1883, anonymously from information provided by Thomas Sissons, a local collector and connoisseur of his work.

110. The painting was given to Trinity House in February 1907 by Alderman Symons. It is not signed and the attribution is traditional. Illustrated in A. Storey *Trinity House of Kingston upon Hull*, Vol.2, p.118. This is the same vessel which appears in John Ward's pictures of the *Swan* and *Isabella*.

111. Ferens Art Gallery.

112. Town Docks Museum, Hull.

113. Robert Willoughby (1768-1843) seems to have devoted nearly all his energies to painting portraits of the ships of the Hull Whaling fleet. Both Willoughby and Ward would no doubt have been influenced by the whaling scene painted by Thomas Fletcher. The latter may well have been Willoughby's master but again the documentary evidence is lacking.

114. Algernon Graves, *A Complete Dictionary of Exhibitors; The Royal Academy of Arts 1769-1904*, Vol.4, London 1905, pp.49-50; John Ward, 103 High Street, item 304, 'Seapiece'.

115. A typescript copy survives in the museum archives. Prices are included for most items.

116. The view expressed by Galloway (1951) that Ward saw Anderson working on the picture *in situ* is totally unfounded. The canvas was a gift to the House in 1813 from Ald. Edward Foster Coulson. See *Naval Chronicle*, 1813, Vol.30, p.3 and Vote Book of the Hull Trinity House, 26th June 1813. The artist's sketchbook of preparatory drawings for this piece is described in the *Mariner's Mirror*, Vol.4, no.8, August 1914 pp.266-74. Its contents were based on eye-witness accounts including sketches provided by Col. Walter Fawkes of the 4th West Yorks. Regiment of Militia.

117. See note 115.

118. For a series of illustrations showing a complete cross-section of Wards output, see A. G. Credland *John Ward of Hull, marine painter, 1798-1849*, Hull, 1981; Catalogue of an exhibition held at the Ferens Art Gallery.

119. Town Docks Museum, Hull.

120. Both works in the Ferens Art Gallery.

121. *Hull Advertiser*, 18 March, 1836.

122. Ferens Art Gallery.

123. *ibid* Joseph Gee was the founder of the Hull Mariners Church Sailors Orphan Society in 1853, Sheriff in 1854 and died in 1860 aged fifty eight.

124. Ferens Art Gallery.

125. The 1841 census records the artist living at 23 North Street, Esther the eldest daughter was thirteen, Sarah Elizabeth ten, Emma seven and Mary Eleanor just one year old. Esther his wife was the daughter of John Leonard, butcher, 116 Union Street, Hull.

126. See above.

127. This project may have been influenced by the example of Dominick and J. T. Serres who in 1805 published their *Liber Nauticus and instructor in the art of marine drawing*. Ward's knowledge of ships was at least equal to theirs and the project if ever it had been completed would have been a classic of nautical illustration.

128. *Hull Advertiser*, 3 February, 1843 (repeated the following month, 3 March).

129. Private Collection.

130. Ferens Art Gallery.

131. Private Collection.

132. *ibid*.

133. A copy of this by J. W. Carmichael is in the Laing Art Gallery, Newcastle.

134. See parish register of Holy Trinity Church, Hull and the *Hull Advertiser*, 5th October, 1849. 'On the 28 ult. after a few hours illness Mr. John Ward, marine painter of this town, deeply lamented by a large circle of friends'.

135. Two collectors of Wards paintings, Charles Spilman Todd, Town Clerk and Michael Wrangles Clarke, Esq., of Winterton Hall were also freemasons and both served terms as Worshipful Masters of the Humber Lodge.

136. *Hull Museum Publications*, no.141, Hull, 1926 pp.44-5 (note that Mr. is used as an abbreviation for marine). A second photograph is preserved in the Local History Library, Hull. A pencil note on the back identifies the sitter as Ward and the artist as (Robert? John?) Willoughby.

137. G. A. Shaw *A History of the Humber Lodge*, Hull, 1909, pp.56-7. It may be noticed that in 1843 Ward gave a lecture to members of the Lodge entitled 'The Theory of Storms and Tempests'. See Anon. *Synopsis of the records of the Humber Lodge, no.57, 1807-1903*, Hull, 1903. Ward presented a portrait of his fellow freemason, Peter Holden to the Humber Lodge on the 23rd June 1846. This was exhibited in 1939-40 but like the self-portrait was lost on the 7th May, 1941, in the blitz which destroyed the Lodge's premises in Anne Street.

138. Towns Docks Museum.

139. See an interview recorded in the *Hull Times*, 22nd February, 1896. Robert Morley Sawyer (1816-1905) was the son of Charles Sawyer (1783-1835), who was for many years captain of the Hull whaleship *Harmony*.

140. It is interesting to note that Settle's father was a nephew of Samuel Ringrose of Cottingham.

141. From about 1834 John Ward lived at 23 North Street, Charlotte Street. The house was at the eastern end of the Street, on the south side, adjacent to Kelseys buildings and the Bethel Chapel; the row terminated with Craggs buildings. All of this area was devastated in the war but is identifiable with the present eastern end of George Street. Craggs buildings was roughly opposite Paradise Row, what is now Carroll Place. In 1846 John Willoughby was sharing number 23 but the following year Ward had moved to number 2 on the north side, near the corner of Bourne Street, and it is this address which is recorded on the front cover of the

English Alphabet. After Wards death in 1849 no.2 was occupied by William Settle's father, Thomas Harris Settle, clerk to the Guardians of the poor, his wife and children.

142. *Hull Advertiser*, 1 May 1802.
143. M.V. and Dorothy Brewington, *The marine paintings and drawings in the Peabody Museum*, Salem, 1968, inv. nos. 1734-6.
144. In the Laing Art Gallery, Newcastle.
145. Lt. Robert Strickland Thomas (1787-1853). Entered the Royal Navy aged eighteen as an able seaman and was shortly after promoted to midshipman; masters mate in the sloop *Brisk* 1807-13; acting lieutenant in the *Creole* at blockade of Cherbourg. Left the service on account of deafness and used his painting skills to supplement half-pay from the navy. Exhibited at the RA 1839 'A Sea Piece', from an address at 6 King Street, Portsea; 1841 'Trafalgar after the close of the action' and 1842 'The Battle of Navarino'.
146. A member of the family of lithographers married Sarah, daughter of C. Appleton of Anlaby near Hull, at the Centenary Chapel, York in 1854; *Hull Advertiser*, 27 May, 1854.

W. F. Settle

147. Baptised at Drypool parish church, 2 April 1821, the eldest son of Thomas Harris Settle and Harriet Leonard.
148. A photograph of Settle as a young man shows a shy and an apparently physically frail individual.
149. The indentures still survive in private hands.
150. In 1840 or 1841; an apprenticeship traditionally takes seven years.
151. Samuel Ringrose lived at 43 George Street, Cottingham ca. 1823-41. Christopher Leake Ringrose occupied Tranby Lodge from 1841 and William Ringrose owned Cottingham Grange in 1842. Previously the latter had lived at Hallgarth House, 270 Hallgate, Cottingham. See K. J. Allison 'Hull Gent, seeks Country Residence, 1750-1850', *East Yorkshire Local History Series, No.36*, 1981.
152. The 1851 census makes it clear that the Settle family were in occupation there, presumably buying or leasing the property from Ward's daughters. The contents of the studio were not sold until 1853.
153. Not the Royal Scottish Yacht Club as reported by Vincent Galloway, *Early Marine Paintings*, Hull, 1951.
154. Probably the house itself was called Ventnor Villa, see below.
155. Not number 2 as indicated in the memoir.
156. He apparently painted this subject several times, see below.
157. Martin Samuelson, shipbuilder and engineer, established a yard on the site of the old citadel in 1854. Long since abandoned for this purpose the spot is still referred to as Sammy's point.
158. Edward Bannister (1821-1916) was apprenticed to John Jacques Matthewson, ornamental painter and fancy chair manufacturer, 9 Junction Street. In July 1844 he set up as a portrait painter at 7 Junction Street. A canvas in the Local History Library is signed and dated 1841 with the inscription 'my first try at oil painting'.
159. He was certainly a patron of William Griffin who painted a number of panels depicting steamers of the Gee fleet and he was a part owner of the *William Lee* so magnificently captured by John Ward.
160. A set of three were sold as lot 234 by Mawer, Mason and Bell of Louth, 21 October, 1980.
161. Private Collection.
162. Private Collection.
163. Present whereabouts unknown.
164. This would have been his earliest dateable work.
165. National Maritime Museum.
166. Private Collection.
167. Ian Basil Settle was his only son; the name Basil is inscribed inside the front page. Some drawings of Norwegian scenery in crayon and watercolour were passed down in the family from Julia Harriet Settle the wife of Robert James McLeavy and daughter of Edwin Thomas Settle, William's younger brother. Edwin was born in 1823 and died in 1878. There were four sisters; Eliza Maria, born 1826; Louisa Harriet, born 1829; Sarah Ann, born 1833; and Caroline, born 1836.
168. See items 15-18; A. G. Credland *John Ward, Marine Artist, op.cit.* item 17, a canvas painting, is probably by Settle.

Henry Redmore

169. The text which follows is an amended version of the essay in the centenary exhibition cata-

logue; A. G. Credland, *Henry Redmore of Hull - Marine Artist 1820-87*, Hull, 1987. The latter includes a series of appendices recording the artists obituary notices in full, works in the collection of the Town Docks Museum and Ferens Art Gallery, local exhibitions to which Redmore contributed and signed and dated works which have passed through the sale rooms.

170. James Redmore married Mary Wilkinson, spinster of Sculcoates, at Holy Trinity Church on the 25th October, 1809, witnessed by Ann Redmore (James' mother) who signed with a cross and John Angelo.

171. *Hull Advertiser*, 5th November, 1847; 'at her residence in Cottingham Terrace aged 65 years, Mary the beloved wife of James Redmore, engineer to Messrs. Mann and Co. of this town'.

172. Obituary notice in the *Hull Arrow*, 15th December, 1887. The magazine was shortlived but the relevant edition is preserved in the Hull Local History Library, Albion Street.

173. *Hull Advertiser*, 24th August and 18th September, 1858, p.4.

174. *Hull Advertiser*, 25th September, 1858.

175. 'Fishing boats, possibly on the Humber estuary, lighthouses centre left', signed and dated 1856, this is a view of Spurn head, *Henry and E. K. Redmore, Sea Paintings*, Lowndes Lodge Gallery, 17th March to 2nd April, 1971. 'Sailing vessels and fishing boats in a fresh breeze off Spurn head', signed H.R. 1857, *Marine Prints, Paintings and Models*, Parker Gallery, 1963, item 804.

176. N.R. Omell Gallery, Duke Street, St. James's, London SW1.

177. Private collection.

178. A. G. Credland, *John Ward of Hull, Marine Painter, 1798-1849*, Hull, 1981, p.p.10-11.

179. *ibid*.

180. Algernon Graves *The Royal Academy of Arts - A complete dictionary of exhibitions*, 1769-1904, 4 volumes, London, 1905:404, 'Fishing ground in the North Sea'; 658 'A Calm on the Humber'; Henry Redmore, painter, Regent Street, Hull; 1868. This was the one hundredth exhibition at the Royal Academy.

181. Lowndes Lodge Gallery 1971, *op.cit*, item 10, 'Steam coaster with the Port of Hull and the tower of Holy Trinity in the background'.

182. *The Hull Arrow*, 15th December, 1887, p.14.

183. An excellent account of the incident appears in the *Scarborough Evening News*, 9th and 10th November, 1978.

184. Oliver Francois Xavier Sarony born in Quebec in 1820 and settled at Scarborough in 1857. After an immensely successful career making studio portraits and cartes de visites he died at Scarborough in 1879. His earnings were said to have reached £10,000 a year (see H. Gernsheim, *The History of Photography*, 1969, p.297 and Beaumont Newhall *The History of Photography*, 1964, p.57).

185. In the collections of the Crescent Art Gallery, Scarborough; there is also a large canvas of the incident ascribed to an artist by the name of Casana. A note in *Contemporary Biographies*, Brighton, 1903, tells us that another well known local artist, Paul Marny, born at Paris 1840 (other sources say 1829) came to Scarborough at the request of Oliver Sarony, the photographer 'for whom he painted "The Shipwreck" in 1861, an oil painting which is probably now in Leeds'.

186. The Carter watercolour is reproduced in Arthur Rowntree - *A History of Scarborough*, 1931. The composition is close to the Redmore pictures described below and another similar watercolour but signed W.C. and dated 1876 is in a private collection at Scarborough. There is also a small oil by J. N. Carter, signed and dated Nov. 13th, 1861, which shows the *Coupland* as the foreground feature with the lifeboat in the distance. The Spa and the spectators are also much less in evidence.

187. *The Hull Arrow, op.cit*.

188. *Hull, Yorkshire and Lincolnshire Fine Arts and Historical Exhibition*, (Public Rooms, Hull) 1883, p.82; item 1172 the 'barque *Canton* abandoned'; 1173 the 'barque *Canton* in a storm'. The lender is listed as the Spring Bank Orphan home, the popular name of the Hull Seamens and General Orphanage before it transferred to Hesslewood.

189. Town Docks Museum.

190. Disposed of in a sale of the contents of the orphanage it was resold as lot 148 in Sotheby's *Marine Sale*, 5th June, 1985.

191. Previously identified by the author as 'Calm on the Humber'; see A. G. Credland, 'Henry Redmore - Marine Artist', *Antique Collecting*, vol.21, Nov. 1986, pp.13-15), this is now

established as 'Hull from the Humber', 1876.

192. They included: George Foster Earle (1813-77) son of George, the co-founder with Thomas of Earles cement works and nephew of Charles and William Earle who established Earles shipyard; Anthony Bannister shipowner and coal exporter and mayor of Hull in 1851 and 1855; James Patrick partner in Hebblethwaite and Patrick 'land agents and surveyors', J. E. Pettingell, solicitor; Joseph Brownridge, surgeon and James Pyburn, surgeon.

193. Probably commissioned by a member of the Gleadow family founders of the Hull Brewery. It was hung at the house of Major R. W. Gleadow Snr. and taken to the attic of the brewery in Silver Street in the 1930's where it was stored until it was hung at the Londesborough Arms Hotel, Market Weighton in about 1960 at the request of Mr. Leslie Cooper one of the directors (information supplied by Mr. Cooper).

194. St. Mary's Sculcoates, 28 November, 1844, witnessed by Jonathan W. Redmore (an uncle?) and Sarah Ann Horsfield.

195. *Hull and Eastern Counties Herald*, 20 June, 1872; Emily was his only surviving daughter.

196. Ann was born 2nd October, 1813 and baptised at Holy Trinity Church on 28 March, 1815; the family were then living in Upper Union Street.

197. The name of Redmore appears in the Hull parish registers long before James settled in Hull though whether there is any relationship has not been established:- e.g. in the Holy Trinity parish registers Martha, daughter of Edward and Sarah Redmore, baptised, 30 January, 1816; Edward Redmore aged 66, buried 25 May, 1817; and John aged 10 son of William Redmore, buried, 10 August, 1827.

198. Thomas was baptised 27 November, 1815, at Holy Trinity Church; the family was then residing in Passage Street; in 1846 they were at Reform Street. See obituary notice, *Hull and Eastern Counties Herald*, 1 August, 1872.

199. *Hull Times*, 1 August, 1885. In the Hull City Record Office a letter is preserved written to Mrs. Redmore on the 24th November, 1875, by C. S. Todd the Town Clerk. Addressed to 8 Cottingham Terrace, it threatened her with a summons unless repairs were completed to 'the pavement and drainage of your premises at Ann's Place, Reform Street' (Board of Health,

B.H.H. 124, p.823).

200. Residents of Regent Street in the 1860's included a large number of clerks, several customs officers, two pilots and a number of gentlemen.

201. As already stated Redmore exhibited at the Academy only in 1868.

202. See *Hull Packet*, 11 July 1879. 'On July 5th at 40 South Parade, Anlaby Road, Hull, in his 39th year, Samuel John Spence, marine and landscape painter'. A note in the museum file records a work in private hands signed S.J.S. with an inscription on the back of the canvas, 'To Capt. Wm. Grandy R.N. from Marquis of Dounshire (sic) Naples, 6th February', it depicts a town wall and a hilly landscape behind and a boat rowed by sailors in the foreground.

203. *The Earle Gallery of Oil Paintings*, put on sale by the executors of G. F. Earle, Esq., and auctioned by Charles Johnson, 'in the large saleroom at the George Hotel, Hull' on Thursday, 26th April, 1877. It was certainly sold in some distinguished company with works by, or attributed to Turner, Constable and Crome as well as Kuyp, Rosa, Lely, and Canaletto: it fetched £15 which may be compared with two marines by J. W. Carmichael which were knocked down for £31 and £22.

204. Hull Temperance Club, *Exhibition of the Work of Local Artists*, April 1881, item 2.

205. I can find nothing to recommend the belief that exists among some dealers and collectors that H. Moore was a pseudonym of Redmore used when he wished to dispose of cheap potboilers.

206. At Holy Trinity Church; the marriage register was witnessed by William Smith and Thomas Hewson. Mrs. Redmore's former husband Alfred Hopwood, is described in the 1863 directory as a gentleman.

207. Ford was still a young man of thirty five in 1881.

208. Five letters; the one written at Regent Street in 1870 already referred to and four others written in 1881-2 were offered for sale at Neales Auction Rooms, Nottingham, 1st May, 1980 and two paintings 'On the Scheldt' (1866) and 'Stormy Seascape' (1867) went under the hammer at the same time. The letters were purchased by the T.D.M. from the Von Braun gallery, Nottingham, in 1985.

209. Lowndes Lodge Gallery, 1971, *op.cit.* items 25 and 26 and Ferens Art Gallery, inv. no. 639, and Town Docks Museum inv. no. M1.1702.
210. *The Hull Arrow*, 15 December, 1887, p.14.
211. See obituary in the *Hull News*, 10 December, 1887.
212. Number 344 in the catalogue: the artists address was given as c/o J. Jackson Esq., Junior Reform Club, Manchester. (Information kindly supplied by Mr. M. Davies, City Art Gallery, Manchester).
213. This is painted on card which during recent cleaning has been lifted from the original canvas base to which it had been glued.
214. Copy preserved in Somerset House.
215. The surviving trustee Robert Buchanan sold th house for £225 to Miss Agnes Mary Clayton, 25 August, 1917; see T.L.A. (F) 34323 Hull City Record Office.

E. K. Redmore
216. Hull Temperance Club, *Exhibition of the work of local artists*, April 1881, item 2.
217. A picture signed E. K. Redmore and inscribed on the reverse 'Homeward bound' was sold as lot 188 at Sothebys, *Marine Sale*, 6th June 1984; 20 by 30 inches.
218. Town Docks Museum, inv. no. M1.1675, watercolour of the Conway Castle off Cape Horn, December 1878; 11 by 15 inches. Gift of Mr. Collins, 59 Rugby Street, Hull in 1969.
219. He died at 4 Crystal Avenue, St. Georges Road, off the Hessle Road, the home of Hull's fishing community. Previously he had occupied 12 Cornwall Gardens, Wheeler Street, also off Hessle Road, and in 1888 was at 41 Day Street, off Great Thornton Street, Anlaby Road.
220. Edward married Catherine Ramster c.1880 and Harold died of consumption 12th September, 1916 whilst working in the munitions industry. There were three other sons Percy, Jack and Kenneth, the latter moved to Liverpool where he joined Elder Dempster the shipping line well known for its trading links with West Africa. In addition there were two daughters Robina and Gladys and the latter was still living in 1987, aged 95.
221. Though he would probably have seen Yarmouth herring drifters at Scarborough.

James Wheldon
222. i.e. marine painter. An oil painting of the sailing ship *Dowthorp* with a Bailey and Leetham steamer in the offing hangs in the Town Docks Museum.
223. The *Diana* is shown with a funnel, i.e. after the installation of a steam engine in 1857, and was wrecked in 1869; the *Chase* sailed to the fishery 1858-60; and the *Abram* from 1844-53.
224. N. R. Omell.
225. The confederate raider *Alabama* and the federal warship *Kearsage* which sank her off Cherbourg in 1864.
226. Wooden screw frigate built at Plymouth 1855 and sold out of the service in 1871.
227. Renamed in 1852 she was previously the *Windsor Castle*.
228. Her successor of that name was a cruiser built by Earles of Hull in 1892.
229. Converted in 1862 from a first rate of 121 guns.
230. Correspondence with Mr. C. F. Green of Kent.
231. If this is the same person baptised in 1832 the age is wrong by a margin of two years, but such discrepancies are common in newspaper obituaries of the period. The *Hull News* 16 June 1900 records thedeath of Alfred Wheldon in his 38th year, youngest son of the late James Wheldon, marine artist.

W. D. Penny
232. He married Louise Jennings, daughter of G. H. Jennings, a cabman, at Holy Trinity Church on 23 July 1877. The witnesses were his father and Edith Maria Penny, the eldest of the three sisters.

James and George Wheldale
233. George Wheldale, painter, married Ann Atkinson at Holy Trinity Church, 3 July, 1836.

R. D. Widdas
234. *Eastern Morning News*, 2 January, 1886.

S. H. Wilson
235. Christies *Maritime Sale*, 13-14 April 1989, lot 47 and lot 46 respectively.

Thomas and Charles Lucop
236. Anon. 'An old Kingston works manager *Ours* (house magazine of Reckitt and Co.) vol.7, no.10, April 1926, pp.556.-6.

Benjamin Tindall

237. The Åland islands form an archipelago at the entrance to the Gulf of Bothnia. Occupied by Russia from 1809 until 1917 when Finland declared its independence. The islands are now an autonomous Swedish-speaking region of Finland.

238. An English owned vessel she traded to America and the United States flag is flying from the foretop. She is depicted off a coastline with a curious castellated structure on a cliff top.

239. *Hull Museums Publications*, 68, Dec. 1909, pp.14-5.

W. R. Nixon

240. Town Docks Museum; M1.316.
241. Town Docks Museum; M1.1483.
242. Town Docks Museum; T1.20.
243. Private Collection.
244. Town Docks Museum; M1.25.

T. J. Somerscales

245. A splendid biography, illustrating many of the works in public and private collections in Chile, has recently been published: Alex A. Hurst, *Thomas Somerscales - marine artist*, Brighton, 1988. See also Patricio Tupper *Som erscales - con el catalogo du su obra*, 1979, Santiago (Chile).

246. Thomas Somerscales (1810-91) died at his home 3 Leicester Street at the age of eighty one; *Eastern Morning News* 23 May 1891.

247. Her full name was apparently Jane Turnbull Harper. She died aged eighty eight, 31 July 1939 at Flackwell Heath, High Wycombe; *Hull Daily Mail* 2 August, 1939.

248. John Somerscales ARCA (1847-1946), died aged ninety nine at 53 Park Avenue, Hull. Diploma student at the Royal College, design master at Manchester School of Art. The mural still survives in what is now the Preston Museum and Art Gallery depicting scenes of Egypt around the walls of the third floor balcony.

249. Francis (Frank) Somerscales designed two cruisers in his career at Earles. His name appears appended to the small etched portraits of Angus Sadler, former Hull whaling captain, and his wife, which appear in the *Hull and East Riding Portfolio*, vol.2, 1885, p.162. He exhibited 'A Devonshire stream' as item 213 in the Hull Fine Art Gallery, Summer exhibition 1889.

250. Anthony North Somerscales, d.1939 at 9 Marlborough Avenue aged eighty eight. Honorary master of the Marine Engineers Association and president of the Hull branch 1904-8. Educated at the Hull Trinity House Navigation School he became the first master of their Adult School which opened in 1872. He opened his own school in 1876 and continued teaching until 1924. A keen model engineer he received the Kensington gold model for steam (*Hull Times*, 29 April, 1939).

251. William Lionel Wyllie (1851-1931) a prolific artist in watercolours and skilful engraver, his oils are very variable in quality; Julius Olsson (1864-1942); born in London he left there in 1896-7 to join the artists colony at St. Ives; a Royal Academician and President of Royal Institute of Oil Painters.

252. Obituaries appeared in the *Hull Daily Mail*, 28 June, 1927; *Yorkshire Post* 2 July, 1927, and the *Hull Times*, 2 July, 1927. As well as the Royal Academy he showed his work at exhibitions of the Royal Society of British Artists, Royal Institute of Oil Painters; also at the Walker Art Gallery and the Manchester Art Gallery.

H.H. Rodmell

253. The text which follows is an amended version of the essay included in the booklet published for the artist's memorial exhibition: A. G. Credland, *Harry Hudson Rodmell - Marine Artist 1896-1984*, Hull, 1984; the latter includes a list of shipping companies for which Rodmell provided posters or other illustrated publicity material and a reprint of 'Getting there' an article illustrated and written by him describing a voyage in the S.S. *Duke of Clarence* from Hull to Zeebrugge, originally published in the *Hull Daily Mail*, 4 April, 1925.

254. *Hull News*, 1919. (precise date omitted from cutting).
255. *Hull News*, 24 August, 1925.
256. *Hull Daily Mail*, 28 January, 1939.
257. *R. C.H.*, 1967, Vol.9, no.1, pp.25-40.
258. *Hull Daily Mail*, 16 June, 1971.

Allanson Hick

259. The text which follows is a precis of the mater-

ial originally published in the booklet accompanying the exhibition at the Town Docks Museum, 7 June-14 July 1991; A. G. Credland (editor and compiler) *Allanson Hick 1898-1975, architect and artist*, Hull, 1991; the biographical information was largely supplied by A. K. Bray and A. G. Chamberlain.

Steven Dews

260. *Hull Daily Mail*, 23 January, 1989.
261. Catalogue of 'Exhibition of Fine Marine Paintings by John Steven Dews' James Starkey Galleries, Beverley, 1976. Twelve subjects are described and illustrated. See also *Hull Daily Mail*, 17 December 1976.
262. A note in the United Towing house magazine *Man to Man*, September, 1977.
263. *Hull Daily Mail*, 10 November 1978.
264. See catalogue of '*The Amoco heritage collection - Famous British Ships, a series of fine marine paintings by J. Steven Dews*'. All twelve subjects are illustrated in colour.
265. *Hull Daily Mail*, 3 February, 1983, p.9; *Yorkshire Post*, 3 February, 1983.
266. *Hull Daily Mail*, 16 March, 1984.
267. *Hull Daily Mail*, 5 February, 1986, p.3; *Yorkshire Post* 13 March, 1986. Sales of the prints based on his original paintings were to raise money to finance entry into the race.
268. *Hull Daily Mail*, 7 June, 1988.
269. *Hull Daily Mail*, 20 November, 1990.
270. *The Journal* (Hull) November 1990; advertisement by Glenn Dunn of S.A.L. Holdings Ltd., Princes Avenue, Hull. Mr. Dunn is now the agent for all Steven Dews work.
271. *Hull Daily Mail*, 20 July, 1989.
272. *Artists and Illustrators Magazine*, January, 1989, pp.20-3.
273. For further biographical notes see *Select* (Beverley) April-May, 1988, pp.20-2; *Seascape* (London) no.18, October 1988, pp.14-11; *The Journal*, (Hull) October 1990, pp.12-3, and *Yachting World*, May 1989, pp.109-11.
274. *The Mid-Ocean News*, 3 May, 1991, p.9.

David Bell

275. The subjects reproduced were P.S. *Lincoln Castle*, 'Humber Bridge', 'Shunting Yard', 'Awaiting the tide' and P.S. *Wingfield castle*. See *Hull Daily Mail*, 10 October, 1981.
276. The Logistics Battalion.
277. The M.V. *Norland* and HMS *Fearless* are depicted under attack in what became known as 'Bomb Alley', '*Hull Daily Mail*', 3 May 1984, p.12.
278. *Hull Daily Mail*, 12 January, 1983.
279. Issued under the auspices of the Hull City Council. See *Hull Daily Mail*, 9 August, 1984.
280. *David Bell - an exhibition of Watercolours*, December 1983, twenty one originals and six lithographs; *The Marine oil paintings of David Bell*, 23 December, 1986.
281. For a brief biographical note see *Lincolnshire Life*, March 1985, p.17.

There are several references to material in the archives of Burton Constable Hall; these documents may be found in the Humberside County Record Office, Beverley, inv. no. DDCC(2).